QlikView Server and Publisher

Deploy and manage QlikView Server and QlikView
Publisher on platforms ranging from a single server to
a multiserver clustered environment

Stephen Redmond

[PACKT] enterprise
PUBLISHING   professional expertise distilled

BIRMINGHAM - MUMBAI

QlikView Server and Publisher

First published: January 2014

Production Reference: 1130114

Published by Packt Publishing Ltd.
Livery Place
35 Livery Street
Birmingham B3 2PB, UK.

ISBN 978-1-78217-985-6

www.packtpub.com

Credits

Author
Stephen Redmond

Reviewers
B. Diane Blackwood

Steve Dark

Brian Diamante

Barry Harmsen

Acquisition Editors
Usha Iyer

Meeta Rajani

Lead Technical Editor
Sharvari Tawde

Technical Editors
Arwa Manasawala

Shali Sasidharan

Copy Editors
Sayanee Mukherjee

Lavina Pereira

Laxmi Subramanian

Project Coordinator
Jomin Varghese

Proofreader
Dirk Manuel

Indexer
Mariammal Chettiyar

Graphics
Ronak Dhruv

Production Coordinators
Manu Joseph

Pooja Chiplunkar

Cover Work
Manu Joseph

Cover Image
Sheetal Aute

About the Author

Stephen Redmond is CTO of CapricornVentis Limited (`http://www.capventis.com`), a QlikView Elite Partner. He is the author of several books, including *QlikView for Developers Cookbook, Packt Publishing*, and the popular DevLogix series for SalesLogix developers.

In 2006, after working for many years with CRM systems, reporting and analysis solutions, and data integration, Stephen started working with QlikView. Since then, CapricornVentis have become QlikView's top partner in the UK and Ireland territory, and with Stephen at the head of the team, they have implemented QlikView in a wide variety of enterprises and large-business customers, across a wide range of sectors, from public sector to financial services to large retailers.

Stephen regularly contributes to online forums, including the Qlik Community. His QlikView blog is at `http://www.qliktips.com`, and you can follow him on Twitter (`@stephencredmond`), where he tweets about QlikView, BI, data visualization, technology in general, and occasionally marathon running.

I would like to thank my family for their ongoing support. None of what I do, would be possible without them.

A big shout out to my colleagues in CapricornVentis who are the best team to work with. I don't think that the world has seen a better team of business solution consultants.

About the Reviewers

B. Diane Blackwood has worked as a consultant implementing **Business Intelligence and Corporate Performance Management (BI and CPM)** solutions since 2005. She is currently employed by Strafford Technology Inc., a Business Intelligence consulting firm (`http://www.strafford.com/Technology/`). She has extensive experience in multiple industries (including micro-electronics, heavy equipment manufacturing, medical, legal, and various retail industries) implementing BI and CPM solutions. In 2010, she worked with El Camino Hospital by creating data warehouse/data marts to feed QlikView, a "social business discovery" software solution. Diane worked closely with Dr. Michael Gallagher, former Director of Informatics at El Camino Hospital, whose enthusiasm for the uses of QlikView in analyzing the hospital and medical data "infected" her.

In 2013, Diane Blackwood wrote *Instant QlikView 11 Application Development*, *Packt Publishing*. Diane has also written several biographic encyclopedia articles, including articles on Charles Babbage, Erving Goffman, and Isaac Asimov.

Thank you to Dr. Michael Gallagher for first showing me the prescribing pattern analysis with QlikView.

Steve Dark was a SQL Server/MS ASP developer, building web-based reporting solutions until he was shown a demo of QlikView. Soon after this epiphany, Steve left his previous employer to set up Quick Intelligence, a consultancy focusing entirely on QlikView and delivering Business Intelligence solutions. Preferring to stay at the coalface, Steve spends the majority of his time with clients by building QlikView applications, managing QlikView deployments, and running projects.

He will be never tired of showing QlikView to new users and seeing that "jaw drop moment". Steve is active on the Qlik Community and other social media sites by sharing his enthusiasm for QlikView and assisting other users. Through his blog he shares tutorials, examples, and insights about QlikView (you can read it at `http://www.quickintelligence.co.uk/qlikview-blog/`).

Steve has been on the technical review team for *QlikView 11 For Developers*, *QlikView 11 For Developers Cookbook* (also by *Stephen Redmond*), and *QlikView Scripting*. All of these titles are published by *Packt Publishing*.

I would like to thank my family for putting up with me being constantly involved in these books and my other QlikView endeavors. Hopefully, my children will at some point, pick up these references and start coding, themselves!

Barry Harmsen is an independent Business Intelligence Consultant based in the Netherlands. Originally from a background of traditional Business Intelligence, data warehousing, and performance management, in 2008 he made the shift to QlikView and a more user-centric form of Business Intelligence.

After switching over to QlikView, Barry has completed many successful implementations in many different industries, ranging from financial services to telecoms, and from manufacturing to healthcare. Barry's QlikView experience covers a wide variety of roles and subjects, including requirements analysis, design, development, architecture, infrastructure, system administration, integration, project management, and training.

In 2012, Barry co-authored the book *QlikView 11 for Developers*, *Packt Publishing*. This book quickly established itself as one of the best ways to teach yourself QlikView. Barry is also one of the core speakers at the Masters Summit for QlikView. This three-day conference for QlikView developers covers advanced topics, and is designed to take your QlikView skills to the next level. More information about Masters Summit can be found at www.masterssummit.com.

Barry writes a QlikView blog at www.qlikfix.com, and can be followed on Twitter via @meneerharmsen.

www.PacktPub.com

Support files, eBooks, discount offers and more

You might want to visit www.PacktPub.com for support files and downloads related to your book.

Did you know that Packt offers eBook versions of every book published, with PDF and ePub files available? You can upgrade to the eBook version at www.PacktPub.com and as a print book customer, you are entitled to a discount on the eBook copy. Get in touch with us at service@packtpub.com for more details.

At www.PacktPub.com, you can also read a collection of free technical articles, sign up for a range of free newsletters and receive exclusive discounts and offers on Packt books and eBooks.

http://PacktLib.PacktPub.com

Do you need instant solutions to your IT questions? PacktLib is Packt's online digital book library. Here, you can access, read and search across Packt's entire library of books.

Why Subscribe?

- Fully searchable across every book published by Packt
- Copy and paste, print and bookmark content
- On demand and accessible via web browser

Free Access for Packt account holders

If you have an account with Packt at www.PacktPub.com, you can use this to access PacktLib today and view nine entirely free books. Simply use your login credentials for immediate access.

Instant Updates on New Packt Books

Get notified! Find out when new books are published by following @PacktEnterprise on Twitter, or the *Packt Enterprise* Facebook page.

Table of Contents

Preface

I have been working with QlikView since 2006. Since I started, the way in which QlikView has been deployed has changed considerably.

Originally, the majority of implementations were individual desktop licenses. There was a user license distinction between Developer, Professional, and Analyzer, with different rights between them. The Developer would create QlikView documents, load data from the database, and then pass over to the Professional to create the UI. The Analyzer user would just open QlikView documents but couldn't edit them.

The QlikView Server was quite a young product. There was also a sister product called QlikView Publisher—but that had a different development cycle and different version numbers. The clients were QlikView Desktop, IE Plugin, Java, and the embryonic Ajax Zero Footprint. The Management Console was a Windows executable file.

Version 8 of QlikView brought the development of Server and Publisher together (well, they had the same version number anyway!). Every deployment of Server could have a "Standard" license of Publisher, which allowed reload tasks only. Enterprise Publisher required a license and had a separate management console. The important thing to note was the improved Ajax ZFC client and the ability to manually generate the HTML code for a site from within QlikView Desktop. That made the QlikView Desktop very easy to deploy and made it a real alternative to the IE plugin. Developers no longer had to enter a license key; they could "Borrow" their user CAL from the server into their client.

Version 9 brought the management of QlikView Server and Publisher together, into a single, web-based management console. Well, actually there were two! The **QlikView Management Console (QMC** — a simplified interface especially for managing single server implementations) and the **QlikView Enterprise Management Console (QEMC** — a more advanced interface especially for managing multiple server deployments). To enable Publisher, you just added the license key, and the Publisher options became available. We no longer had to manually generate the HTML for the Ajax ZFC. You just needed to deploy the QVW and it would appear in the AccessPoint; if a user opened it, the HTML was generated automatically. Licensing also changed, and we got rid of the old Developer/Professional/Analyzer licenses and replaced them with just the Named User license, which you borrow (although now renamed to "Lease") from the server. Document licenses were introduced later.

Version 10 brought some great performance improvements, and a new skin for QMC and QEMC. There were also some advancements made in APIs that allowed the development of applications that made calls to the Management Service to retrieve information — this was the genesis of the power tools. Extension objects for the Ajax client were introduced. The old Java client was dropped. Service releases later saw the Ajax client become gesture-aware so that it could be used on iPads and Android devices.

Version 11, the current version, got rid of QMC and just uses QEMC, although this has actually been renamed as QMC! There were many great improvements, including a really good re-design of the Ajax views. The Ajax ZFC client is now a valid default client for organizations. Other features for the Ajax client, such as session collaboration, are not available in other clients. Document extensions have been introduced.

I feel lucky, in a way, that we started selling QlikView at that time when more deals started to include QlikView Server instead of standalone implementations. Now, more than 100 implementations later, almost all of them have been server based. We have implemented all of the options across our various clients, and have hit, and resolved, many roadblocks along the way.

In this book, short as it is, I have tried to distill as much of the knowledge gathered over all those years into these pages. I hope that you find it useful.

What this book covers

Chapter 1, Getting Started with QlikView Server, begins the journey with details of the supported Windows platforms for the QlikView Server, the things that you are going to need to consider before implementation, the hardware considerations, the different types of licenses available, and the deployment options.

Chapter 2, Standard Installation Process, goes step-by-step through a standard installation of QlikView Server, where all components are installed on one box.

Chapter 3, Exploring the QlikView Management Console in Detail, introduces us to the QMC, the main management tool that we use with QlikView Server and other QlikView services.

Chapter 4, Managing and Securing QlikView Documents, looks at different methods of securing QlikView documents as well as some of the other properties that we can manage via the QMC.

Chapter 5, Installing QlikView Server Enterprise, walks through a full implementation of QlikView Server services on multiple servers, including implementing a QlikView Server Cluster.

Chapter 6, Configuring the QlikView Publisher, explains how to configure options for QlikView Publisher and how to create a trigger reload and other tasks.

Chapter 7, Alternative Authentication and Authorization Methods, goes through the different options for authentication beyond Active Directory, by using QlikView's DMS authentication models, including LDAP, HTTP header, and Custom Ticket Exchange (CTE).

Chapter 8, Monitoring and Troubleshooting QlikView Server, reviews the log files that you need to know about in order to monitor the services and resolve issues, and also looks at some of the tools available to help you administer the QlikView Server.

What you need for this book

You need to have a server or PC that is capable of running QlikView Server (refer to *Chapter 1, Getting Started with QlikView Server*, for details). You will need access to the QlikView Downloads site or know someone who does (for example, a QlikView Partner), and have some kind of license for QlikView Server.

If you are not an existing customer of QlikView, you won't have access to the downloads or have a license. In that case, you will need to engage with a QlikView Partner to access the files and to obtain an evaluation license for QlikView Server.

Who this book is for

If you are a server administrator willing to learn about how to deploy QlikView Server for server management, analysis and testing, and use QlikView Publisher for publishing of business content, then this is the perfect book for you. No prior experience with QlikView is necessary.

Conventions

In this book, you will find a number of styles of text that distinguish between different kinds of information. Here are some examples of these styles, and an explanation of their meaning.

Code words in text, database table names, folder names, filenames, file extensions, path names, dummy URLs, user input, and Twitter handles are shown as follows: "To get a "clean" uninstall, we can uninstall and then manually delete the `ProgramData\QlikTech` folder."

A block of code is set as follows:

```
Option Explicit

' Establish some variables
Dim sServer, sSuccessURL, sFailURL
Dim sUser, sGroups, sGroupList
Dim sURL, sRequest, sResult, sTicket
Dim iStart
```

Any command-line input or output is written as follows:

```
QMSEDX.exe -task="Sales Analysis.qvw" -pwd=mypassword
```

New terms and **important words** are shown in bold. Words that you see on the screen, in menus or dialog boxes for example, appear in the text like this: "The QlikView Desktop has the option to **Open in Server** and connect to a QlikView Server to open a document."

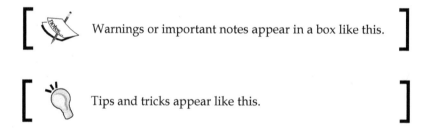

> Warnings or important notes appear in a box like this.

> Tips and tricks appear like this.

Reader feedback

Feedback from our readers is always welcome. Let us know what you think about this book—what you liked or may have disliked. Reader feedback is important for us to develop titles that you really get the most out of.

To send us general feedback, simply send an e-mail to feedback@packtpub.com, and mention the book title via the subject of your message.

If there is a topic that you have expertise in and you are interested in either writing or contributing to a book, see our author guide on www.packtpub.com/authors.

Customer support

Now that you are the proud owner of a Packt book, we have a number of things to help you to get the most from your purchase.

Downloading the example code

You can download the example code files for all Packt books you have purchased from your account at http://www.packtpub.com. If you purchased this book elsewhere, you can visit http://www.packtpub.com/support and register to have the files e-mailed directly to you.

Errata

Although we have taken every care to ensure the accuracy of our content, mistakes do happen. If you find a mistake in one of our books—maybe a mistake in the text or the code—we would be grateful if you would report this to us. By doing so, you can save other readers from frustration and help us improve subsequent versions of this book. If you find any errata, please report them by visiting http://www.packtpub.com/submit-errata, selecting your book, clicking on the **errata submission form** link, and entering the details of your errata. Once your errata are verified, your submission will be accepted and the errata will be uploaded on our website, or added to any list of existing errata, under the Errata section of that title. Any existing errata can be viewed by selecting your title from http://www.packtpub.com/support.

Piracy

Piracy of copyright material on the Internet is an ongoing problem across all media. At Packt, we take the protection of our copyright and licenses very seriously. If you come across any illegal copies of our works, in any form, on the Internet, please provide us with the location address or website name immediately so that we can pursue a remedy.

Please contact us at copyright@packtpub.com with a link to the suspected pirated material.

We appreciate your help in protecting our authors, and our ability to bring you valuable content.

Questions

You can contact us at questions@packtpub.com if you are having a problem with any aspect of the book, and we will do our best to address it.

1
Getting Started with QlikView Server

At a simple level, QlikView Server is a product that serves QlikView documents to connected users.

Users connect to AccessPoint — the out of the box QlikView web portal — and see their documents. They click on a document and it opens, displaying their up-to-date data.

Of course, under the hood, it is a lot more complex than that. There are multiple services in action. The main one is the QlikView Server service that actually loads the documents into memory on the server and delivers the information to clients. The QlikView Web Server service hosts AccessPoint and renders the QlikView documents to web and mobile clients. The Directory Service connector allows QlikView to connect to different user repositories and the QlikView Management service links everything together.

Up-to-date data is important to users, so we have the QlikView Distribution Service. Without a QlikView Publisher license, this is a simple reload engine that reloads the documents on a schedule. After adding the Publisher license, the Distribution Service becomes a service that reloads documents and distributes them to multiple locations with multiple options and schedules.

Before you begin to think about installing QlikView Server, there are some important things that you should know. We will cover them all in this chapter.

When you install the product, you are going to need some hardware in place — either physical or virtual — so you will need to understand the implications of different configurations and sizes.

Because QlikView is built on a **Service Oriented Architecture (SOA)**, we will also look at the architecture of the different services so that you might understand how many servers you might need to deploy.

We will also look at the different licenses that you can use with QlikView Server and the different client types that can be deployed.

These are the topics we'll be covering in this chapter:

- Supported Windows Servers
- Licensing and Server types
- Deployment options
- Service Oriented Architecture
- QlikView clients

Supported Windows Servers

QlikView is a Windows-based technology. Up to Version 11.2 SR4, there have been both 32-bit and 64-bit versions of QlikView Server (and Publisher).

These versions can be installed on the following Windows Server versions:

- Windows Server 2003, both 32-bit and 64-bit
- Windows Server 2003 R2, both 32-bit and 64-bit
- Windows Server 2008, both 32-bit and 64-bit
- Windows Server 2008 R2 (64-bit only)

For purposes of testing and development only, QlikView Server 32-bit or 64-bit can also be installed on the following professional (not home edition) desktop operating systems:

- Windows XP, both 32-bit (SP3) and 64-bit (SP2)
- Windows Vista, both 32-bit and 64-bit
- Windows 7, both 32-bit and 64-bit

Essentially, this is the list of operating systems that support the Microsoft .NET Framework 4.0, which is required by QlikView Server.

Since version 11.2 SR2, an additional installation is available specifically for Windows 2012. This version will also install on Windows 8, for test and development purposes only.

QlikView Server will install on a fairly barebones Windows Server. The only additional requirement is an installation of the Microsoft .NET Framework — v4 for QlikView v11 and v11.2. If the .NET Framework is not installed when you start the QlikView Server installation, the QlikView installer will attempt to start the download and installation process for it.

Of course, this means that if the server is not connected to the Internet, the download will fail.

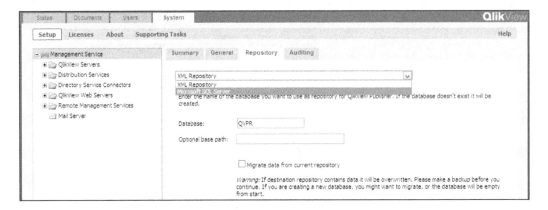

The installation will automatically create the **QVPR** (this is a legacy from the **QlikView Publisher Repository**, but it is not just about publisher any longer), an XML file-based storage of server settings managed by the QlikView Management service. Because these XML files are potentially corruptible on the filesystem, some administrators would prefer to have them stored in a more robust database. There is an option in the QlikView Management Console, to migrate the QVPR to SQL Server. This SQL Server could be running on the same server as the QlikView services but it is not recommended, as it will consume resources that might be needed by QlikView. It is worth noting that if you keep using the XML repository, the XML files will be backed up to ZIP files on either a daily basis or on a schedule that you can configure.

Other Windows options that you need to consider

There are a number of other Windows options that you need to consider before deploying QlikView Server.

IIS

To run the QlikView AccessPoint, QlikView Server has its own web server service—**QlikView Web Service/Settings Service (QVWS)**. However, it will also deploy on IIS v6, v7, or v8 (on Windows 8/2012). This may be the preferred option for many IT departments, especially if they have existing IIS management experience or need to easily manage security certificates.

Authentication

The default security model uses either NTLM or Kerberos to authorize either an Active Directory or local SAM user. This default is the only option available for the Small Business Edition of QlikView Server. Other authentication mechanisms are possible with Enterprise QlikView Server (refer to *Chapter 7, Alternative Authentication and Authorization Methods*), so you will need to consider security.

Browser

The **QlikView Management Console** (**QMC**) is a web-based tool that you will need a "modern" web browser to work with—so IE6 won't work. This doesn't need to be on the server, but it is useful to have it there. The following browsers are suitable:

Browser	Minimum Version
Internet Explorer	7
Google Chrome	18
Mozilla Firefox	12
Apple Safari	5

I have used all of these browsers and although I have a personal preference for Google Chrome, all of them should work fine. You will have to watch out if using IE on your server because the enhanced security option is often enabled. In these circumstances, I have sometimes found myself having to download Firefox (because IE blocks the Chrome download!)

Internet Protocol

The Internet Protocol is not something that you might consider normally because it is set by default in Windows Server, but some organizations may have IP turned off. QlikView services talk to each other using the HTTP protocol, so it is important that IP is available—either IPv4 or IPv6.

Print spooler service

The print spooler service is necessary for QlikView to generate reports for web-based users. In fact, if it is disabled, the PDF-XChange drivers that QlikView uses will not even install. Unfortunately, it is common for IT departments to disable this service as part of Group Policy. Check that this is enabled before installation.

Windows hardware considerations

Windows Servers have their own hardware requirements but going with a minimum option will not work for QlikView. QlikView Server is a CPU- and memory-intensive application. You will need to have enough of both to be able to handle your data and your user requirements (refer to the *Ready reckoner* section).

Because QlikView Server is so hardware intensive, it is rarely appropriate to host the QlikView Server on a server that will also host other services such as Microsoft SQL Server, Microsoft Exchange Server, and so on. By default, QlikView Server will consume up to 90 percent of the available physical RAM on the server and that doesn't leave much for other services.

Memory

It is worth remembering that a 32-bit Windows process can only access a maximum of 2 GB of memory. So, if you are running a 32-bit QlikView Server, there would be little point in having more than 4 GB of memory. On the other hand, if you are running 64-bit Windows, 4 GB would be an absolute minimum! I wouldn't normally recommend a 32-bit server for QlikView. Since Windows 2008 R2, there is no longer a 32-bit version of Windows Server.

There is no hard and fast rule on the amount of memory that you will need for your implementation, as it is dependent on the amount of data that you will be loading, the number of applications that will be used, the number of users who will be accessing those applications, and how often they will be accessing them. It is also worth considering that the amount of data and the number of applications will likely increase over time.

CPU

QlikView loads the data from the documents into memory, but every time a user makes a different selection, all of the data needs to be recalculated by QlikView's chart engine. You will need enough CPU power to be able to process these calculations in good time, for both user experience and to avoid time-outs. For most calculations, QlikView Server scales linearly across CPU cores. If you double the number of cores that you have, the calculations will mostly be calculated twice as fast.

There is a memory partitioning scheme known as NUMA, which allocates blocks of memory to a particular processor on the basis that this processor can access that area of memory quicker than areas assigned to other processors. Because QlikView applications can be in larger blocks of memory, and because the calculations execute across all processors, this scheme can actually end up degrading performance of the QlikView Server. Therefore, non-NUMA or Interleaved memory partitioning schemes should be used.

Ready reckoner

The following table can be used as a very rough estimate for the size of server that you might need. When considering the number of **Fact** rows (lowest level transactions) and number of users, you should consider all of the expected applications and allow an increase over time.

It is very important to remember that every dataset is different and there are many things that make up the size of a QlikView application. The best approach is to use the following table as a rough estimate but also to add the ability to increase if necessary:

Number of "Fact" rows	Number of users (Concurrent)	Servers	CPU cores	Memory
10,000,000	20 (5)	1	8	8 GB
10,000,000	100 (20)	1	16	16 GB
50,000,000	20 (5)	1	16	32 GB
100,000,000	100 (20)	1	16	64 GB
800,000,000	200 (50)	1	16	128 GB
800,000,000	400 (100)	1	24	256 GB
800,000,000	1000 (200)	2	24	256 GB
2,000,000,000	4000 (400)	4	24	512 GB

Virtualization

QlikView Server works well on a VM. For many years now, VMWare has been "officially" supported, but I have also implemented it on Citrix XEN. The QlikView Demo servers are hosted on Amazon EC2 servers (a variation of XEN). Essentially, QlikView Server is a Windows application, and so will run on Windows, including virtualized servers.

Having said that, we need to be aware that QlikView is an intensive user of the hardware on the server. There will be a performance hit on a virtual server because of the overhead of the hypervisor. The nature of QlikView Server's use of hardware is that it tends to require memory and CPU in intensive bursts. This does not work well with virtual servers with any type of shared resource or ballooning. If there is any significant latency when QlikView Server tries to access resources, the service can crash. For this reason, resources assigned to a QlikView Server should be reserved for that server.

Licensing and Server types

There are four types of server licenses and user licenses available. There are different restrictions of the latter type, depending on the former type.

The pricing given in this section is as it was at the time of writing this book but this information is publicly available from the QlikView website: http://www. qlikview.com/us/explore/pricing.

Client licenses

There are four client access license types. We will discuss these in detail, shortly.

Named User license

The **Named User** license is, as its name suggests, a client access license that is associated with a particular user. This is the most flexible of the license types from the perspective of document access. A named user can open as many server documents as they have access to.

The named user also has the option of leasing their license from the server to a copy of QlikView Desktop. This allows them to open and create QVW files locally. Essentially, this is the license that you will assign to developers and power users—those that will access multiple documents.

At the time of this writing, a Named User license costs $1,350.

Document license

The **Document** license is, again, a Named User license. However, it restricts the named user to one named QlikView document. One named user can be assigned one license each for multiple documents and each document can have licenses for multiple users.

At $350 per license (at the time of this writing), this can be a cost-effective way of getting one application out to many users. While that may sound expensive compared to some other products, it is worth noting that a Document license user can still create their own content within the context of the document.

The ratio of just under 4:1 between the cost of Document license and Named User license means that, if any of your users require access to four or more documents, then a Named User license would be more cost effective than multiple Document licenses. Indeed, many customers will deploy Named User licenses to avoid the potential hassle of managing the association of user to document.

Concurrent license

The **Concurrent** license, formerly called a Session CAL, doesn't have a restriction on the number of users or documents; instead the restriction is on the number of concurrent sessions — one license equals one concurrent session. A session corresponds to one user accessing the server for a period of 15 minutes. Within that 15-minute period, the user could open multiple documents but still remain within that "session". If they are still active at the end of those 15 minutes, they keep hold of that session and begin a new 15-minute period.

This is a very flexible license type when you have a large population of users who will be accessing documents in a very ad hoc kind of way. It wouldn't really be suitable for users who are going to use one or more documents for longer periods. A Concurrent license (at the time of this writing) costs $15,000, which is a cost ratio of 11.11:1 versus the Named User license. A single user who is consuming many sessions should probably be assigned either a Named User license or Document license instead.

Usage license

A **Usage** license corresponds to one user using one document for one hour in any one 28-day period. They are generally sold in blocks of 100. As each user uses a license, the number reduces down to zero but then resets back each month.

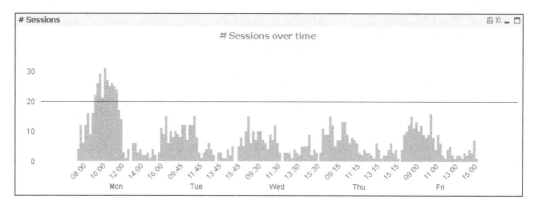

This is an interesting license type that is usually associated with the Concurrent license. To describe it, imagine that you have 20 Concurrent users and this perfectly suits your usage profile Tuesday to Friday. However, it is Monday morning when everyone is trying to get their sales figures for the last week. 20 users are already in and a 21st user tries to access the server—he won't get in as all of the sessions are being consumed. This is where a Usage license comes in. As the 21st and the 22nd user hit the server, they get assigned a Usage license instead, and they can carry on with their analysis. It complements a population of Concurrent users, to cover those periods of overuse on the concurrency.

QlikView Small Business Edition Server license

The **Small Business Edition** (**SBE**) Server is a fully-functional QlikView Server that is designed to sit on one server only and has a limit on the number of users that can be licensed.

Each of the QlikView services—QlikView Server, Distribution Service (reloads), Management Server, and so on—will sit on the same server. This is different from a more "enterprise" deployment, where the various services can be deployed on different servers.

There is a limitation on the license types available. There is a maximum of 25 Named User licenses and 100 Document licenses allowed on SBE. Concurrent and Usage licenses are not allowed.

At the time of this writing, a Small Business Edition Server license costs $8,400 per server.

QlikView Enterprise Edition Server license

This is the license that most large organizations will deploy. QlikView Enterprise has no limitations on the number of Named User or Document licenses and allow Concurrent and Usage licenses. We can also introduce server clustering.

Each of the Services can be deployed on a separate server (although it is not compulsory!).

Additional server licenses can be added to scale the solution by using QlikView clustering.

At the time of this writing, an Enterprise Edition Server license costs $35,000 per server. The per-server price includes either multiple standalone servers or clustered servers.

QlikView Extranet Server license

The Extranet Server is designed to present data to people who are external to your organization. It is limited in that you can only deploy Concurrent licenses. These are specially priced (at the time of writing) at $3,000 (rather than $15,000 for the normal Concurrent license).

At the time of this writing, an Extranet Server license costs $18,000 per server.

QlikView Information Access Server license

This is a special QlikView Server license that allows unlimited user access to one QlikView document. As such, there are no user licenses associated with it. All of the users must be anonymous and, as such, you can't secure the data to users, and it must be open to all users. The website must be available publicly with no authentication. This is an ideal license for delivering information to the public using QlikView's excellent user interfaces.

At the time of this writing, an Information Access Server license costs $70,000 per server.

QlikView Publisher license

Without QlikView Publisher, the QlikView Distribution Service can only work alongside QlikView Server to perform reloads of documents in the server folders. The reload task can only have one trigger — the event that starts the reload — associated with it. The trigger can be a time-based event (daily, hourly, weekly, and so on), it could be an event from another reload (success or failure), or it could be an externally triggered event — **EDX** (**Event Diven eXecution**).

Once the Publisher license has been added, the Distribution Server can be deployed on its own server and can perform a much wider range of tasks including reloads, reduction of data in documents based on selections in the document, distribution of documents to multiple locations, and execution of external tasks. Each of these tasks can have multiple triggers and multiple dependencies (a dependency means that the execution of another task must have completed successfully prior to this task being started). It also introduces the additional server management option of having document administrators and the publisher authorization portal. The document administrators can be given the rights to administer a particular server folder. This includes changing document settings and reloads. The publisher authorization portal allows you to create mapping tables that are stored on the publisher server. The design purpose of these is to implement Section Access tables, but they can actually be used for any lookup tables that you might need.

At the time of this writing, a QlikView Publisher license costs $21,000 per server. As with QlikView Server, QlikView Publishers can also be clustered.

For an additional $21,000, you can add the functionality to distribute PDF files generated from QlikView reports in a QlikView document.

Deployment options

There are five services that make up a QlikView Server deployment:

- **QlikView Management Service (QMS)**: The QlikView Management Service talks to all of the other services to set up their configurations and manage tasks. It also publishes an API that external applications can use to interact with the QlikView Server deployment.
- **QlikView Server (QVS)**: The QlikView Server service is the core engine of QlikView when deployed on a server. It loads the QVW documents into memory, performs the necessary calculations to present the correct results, and handles user and document memory allocation.

- **QlikView Directory Service Connector (DSC)**: The Directory Service Connector is the service that connects to different user repositories, such as Active Directory, LDAP, or even a custom database of users, to allow configuration of document-level security.

- **QlikView Distribution Service (QDS)**: Without a publisher license, the Distribution Service is simply a reload engine, reloading QVW documents on a QlikView Server. With the Publisher license added, it becomes an independent service that can perform reloads anywhere, distribute documents to multiple locations, and can perform many more tasks.

- **QlikView Web Service/Settings Service (for IIS) (QVWS)**: QlikView supports deploying its web pages on IIS but also comes with its own web server service—QVWS. If you do deploy on IIS, the Settings Service acts like the QVWS (listening on the same ports) and communicates with IIS to configure the correct settings.

Each of the services maintains their own folder and file structures, and they can all be enabled for SNMP if required.

There are several common deployment options, which we will discuss in the forthcoming sections.

Single server

This is a very common option for many customers—especially for the so-called "departmental" implementations. You have one server and all of the services are deployed on that server.

Obviously, this is the easiest option to deploy and it works quite well. It is also the only option available for the SBE server.

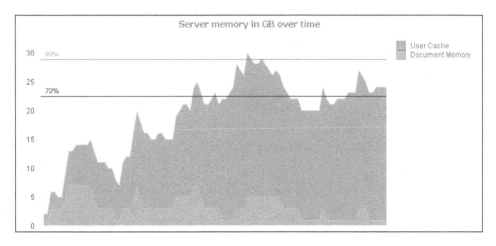

Problems only start to arise where there is a scarcity of memory. The QVS will grab as much system memory as it can, up to about 90 percent of physical RAM (this is configurable), and will tend to hang on to allocated memory, especially user cache, once it has taken it. Any reload task will use memory as needed, and that could be a lot of memory if there are complex script processes. If there are reloads happening during the day, the server will come under resource pressure, which can cause errors, failures, and unhappy users.

Server/Publisher

In this option, which requires a Publisher license, the Distribution Service is deployed on a separate server to the one on which the QVS and other services are deployed. The Publisher server doesn't need to have the same hardware specification as the larger QVS server. Because memory and CPU resources are released when each task is completed, the server only needs enough resources to complete those tasks – it doesn't hold the resource like QVS does.

Enterprise

An Enterprise deployment will require multiple servers with different services running on each. It will also normally have multiple QVS servers using QlikView Cluster technology. An example configuration might be similar to the one shown in following diagram:

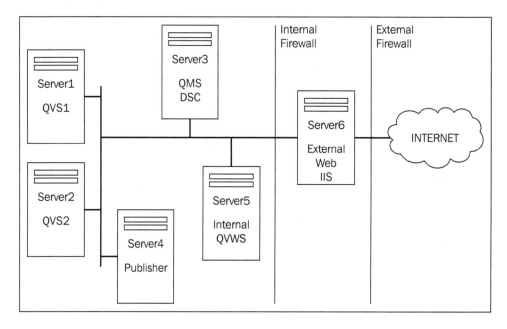

The various Servers shown in the previous diagram and their corresponding services are listed in the following table:

Server	Services
Server 1	QVS1
Server 2	QVS2
Server 3	QMS, DSC
Server 4	QDS (Publisher)
Server 5	QVWS (or IIS)
Server 6	QVWS (or IIS)

The Publisher server can also be clustered, in order to extend the resilience of the deployment.

The web servers can also be deployed in a, so-called, **DMZ** (a security zone, protected by network firewalls that allows people on the Internet to connect to the web server but not to get any direct access to the QlikView Server) to provide the ability to publish QlikView data externally.

Service Oriented Architecture

All of the QlikView services talk to each other using HTTP web service calls. This means that the services can be easily deployed on different servers—even in different domains and behind firewalls—as long as the services can make calls on the ports they use.

QlikView Server

The QVS is slightly different from the other servers, in that "direct" clients—QlikView Desktop, QlikView Plugin, and any OCX clients—will communicate with it via a proprietary, encrypted, binary messaging format, QVP, over port 4747. If a client can't connect directly with the server on port 4747, they have the option of "tunneling" via HTTP or HTTPS through the QVWS or IIS; the web server then talks to QVS over port 4774. The Ajax and mobile clients do not go directly to the QVS. They will communicate to the QVWS/IIS using the XML-based QVPX format.

The QlikView Server also has a settings port 4749, which is available when using certificates. QVS listens for SNMP queries on port 161.

QlikView Management service

This service is the main broker between the other services. It presents the **QlikView Management Console** (**QMC**) to administrators on port 4780. The URL is as follows:

`http://servername:4780/QMC/SystemSetup.htm`

This is the frontend that an administrator can use to set up and configure all of the QlikView services. The QMC requires NTLM authentication, and only members of the local QlikView Administrators Group can run the console.

QMS also has a backend service address on port 4799 that allows access to the API via the web service address `http://servername:4799/QMS/Service`.

The web services can be accessed by users who are members of the local QlikView Management API group.

If enabled, QMS listens for SNMP queries on port 4781.

QlikView Web Server/Settings service

The QVWS service will serve web pages over port 80 (HTTP) or 443 (HTTPS) or any other configurable port. When listening for requests from other services, such as QMS, it listens on port 4750. The service address is `http://servername:4750/QVWS/Service`.

If the QVWS is deployed in a different firewall segment to the QMS, you will need to ensure that port 4750 is open in both directions. Similarly, port 4747 needs to be open in both directions between the QVWS/IIS and QVS.

If enabled, QVWS listens for SNMP queries on port 4751.

Directory Service Connector

The DSC is the service that connects to user repositories such as Active Directory or LDAP. It communicates on port 4750. The service address is `http://servername:4730/DSC/Service`.

As with other services, if this is located on a different firewall segment, port 4730 will need to be open in both directions between the servers.

If enabled, the QDS listens for SNMP queries on port 4731.

QlikView Distribution Service

The QlikView Distribution Service is the service that enables the QlikView Publisher functionality. It listens on port 4720. The service address is `http://servername:4720/QDS/Service`.

This service is only available if there is a QlikView Publisher license installed. As with the other services, port 4720 will need to be open to enable communication across a firewall.

If enabled, QDS listens for SNMP queries on port 4721.

QlikView clients

There are several ways of connecting and consuming QlikView Server data. We will discuss the main clients in the forthcoming sections.

QlikView Desktop Client

The QlikView Desktop Client has the option to **Open in Server** and connect to a QlikView Server to open a document. This defaults to using Windows authentication, and the user's Windows credentials are automatically passed through to QVS. By navigating to **File | Open in Server**, or by using the **Show Options** selection from the **Open in Server** option on the **Start Page**, the user can specify alternative credentials.

By default, all Desktop clients will have a Personal Edition license. This means that they can create new content but cannot share it with other Personal Edition licensed users. If a user opening a server document has a Named User license, and the server is configured to allow leasing, the license will be leased to the Desktop client. The status will change from Personal Edition to **QlikView User License (using license lease from server)**. The user will now be able to create new content that can be shared with other licensed users. This license is leased for 30 days at a time. Every time you run the QlikView Desktop executable, it will try and refresh the lease for a further 30 days. If you have been disconnected from the server for more than 30 days, it will revert to Personal Edition.

It is also possible to obtain a standalone license key that can be entered into the QlikView Desktop client by navigating to **Settings | User Preferences**. This user will then be able to create content, but this license will not license them to open a document from the server — they would still require a server-based license to do that.

QlikView Plugin Client

The QlikView Plugin Client is an ActiveX container of the QlikView OCX control that is only available within Internet Explorer.

An AccessPoint user can choose the **Internet Explorer Plugin** as either their default or on a document-by-document basis. This will also integrate with alternative authentication mechanisms such as **Custom Ticket Exchange** (CTE).

A user can also choose to bypass AccessPoint and attempt to access the QVS directly via the plugin by using a URL in the form:

```
http://servername/QvPlugin/opendoc.htm?document=Movies%20Database.qvw
```

This URL can also have a **Custom Ticket Exchange** (CTE) ticket appended to it for integration with alternative authentications. Refer to *Chapter 7, Alternative Authentication and Authorization Methods*, for more information on CTE.

The same QlikOCX control used by the QlikView Plugin Client can be used within other Windows applications as a COM control and is commonly used by OEMs to deploy QlikView within their solution.

QlikView Ajax Zero Footprint Client

Probably becoming the default option for most new customers, the AjaxZfc client can be deployed with no client-side installation and will work well in a wide variety of browsers — including mobile browsers that are found on the iPad, iPhone, and Android devices. It uses HTML5 and Ajax technology to present a high-quality client to users. It is "touch aware" for mobile clients.

While it is not perfect, it is very much a What-You-See-Is-What-You-Get when compared with the "thicker" Desktop/Plugin clients.

As with the plugin client, a user can also choose to bypass AccessPoint and attempt to access the document directly by using a URL of the form:

```
http://servername/QvAjaxZfc/opendoc.htm?document=Movies%20Database.qvw
```

A CTE ticket can also be appended to this URL for use with alternative authentications. Refer to *Chapter 7, Alternative Authentication and Authorization Methods*, for more information on CTE.

QlikView iPad App

The latest incarnation of the QlikView iPad App is basically a container for the AjaxZfc client. It has some nice features for managing single sign-on for users into the AccessPoint equivalent. It also has a limited "offline" mode that allows a user to store a specific set of selections for offline viewing without having a live connection to the QlikView Server. It is available for free from the Apple App Store.

Summary

In this chapter, we have learnt about all of the supported versions of Microsoft Windows server that QlikView will run on. We have discussed the different types of licensing and QlikView Server types. We have also reviewed some different deployment options. Then, we looked at how the different QlikView services communicate in a QlikView's Service Oriented Architecture. Finally, we went through all of the QlikView clients that can consume information from QlikView Server.

In the next chapter, we will look at preparing for and then installing QlikView Server in a default configuration.

2
Standard Installation Process

The default installation of QlikView Server is very straightforward. As compared to the earlier versions, it is safe to say that it is "easy".

In this chapter, we will step through the default installation process, where all of the services will reside on a single Windows Server. Even if your deployment is spread across multiple servers, there are valuable lessons to learn here, and you may even use this installation on a test/development server.

These are the topics we'll be covering in this chapter:

- Preparing the QlikView environment; this includes:
    - Service account
    - Microsoft .NET Framework 4.0
    - Connectivity
    - Obtaining the QlikView software
- Installing the QlikView Server step-by-step
- Testing the implementation

Preparing the QlikView environment

Before we start installing QlikView Server, there are a number of things that we need to prepare.

Service Account

All of the QlikView services require a user account to run the service, as opposed to using the local system account. This will be a normal domain user, who will be granted membership to the **Local Administrators** group on each of the QlikView servers.

 It is actually possible to use a local account for the service user when running all of the QlikView services on the same server. However, this user would have difficulty in accessing network resources such as file shares and SQL servers. Also, if you decide later to move some services onto a new server, you could have authentication issues. For these reasons, I would always recommend that you to use a domain account.

In the examples in this book, I will use a user called QvService.

During installation, the process will create a **QlikView Administrators** group on the local **Security Account Manager (SAM)** database. The user who is running the installation will be added to this group automatically. Later, we will see how we can specify the service account user during installation—the service account will also be added to the **QlikView Administrators** group.

In a normal installation process, the **QlikView Administrators** group is used for two things:

- Authenticating administrator users to the **QlikView Management Console (QMC)**
- Authenticating the service account user when services are communicating with each other

You can use the standard Windows administration tools to add additional users to this group, to give them the authority to access the QMC.

Microsoft .NET Framework 4.0

QlikView 11.x requires that the Microsoft .NET Framework be installed prior to any QlikView service being installed. If it is not detected while running the installer, the Web installer for it will be launched. However, as servers are not always connected to the Internet—there may be proxy or firewall restrictions in place—my advice would be to download the standalone installer from Microsoft, and install it before starting the QlikView installation process. At the time of this writing, the download site was:

```
http://www.microsoft.com/en-ie/download/details.aspx?id=17718
```

This will download a file called `dotNetFx40_Full_x86_x64.exe`, which contains the full installation process, and it will work on both 32 bit and 64 bit platforms.

Connectivity

If you don't have a Publisher license, then the reloads will generally be performed on the server, and the server will require OLEDB, ODBC, or custom (for example, SAP Netweaver or SalesForce.com) drivers that are necessary to connect to the data sources. If you have a Publisher license, the drivers will need to be installed on the Publisher's server.

If your data source is SQL Server, there are both OLEDB and ODBC drivers installed with all versions of Windows. However, it is recommended to install the latest version of the SQL Server client software.

Some companies prefer to have reloads performed on a separate desktop by using QlikView Desktop Client with a command-line-batch file, and running them with either the Windows scheduler or a third-party one. In that case, the necessary drivers should be installed on that desktop.

 It is worth noting that if you do use QlikView Desktop to execute reloads, you may lose some of the nice server features, such as creating alerts and central management. Where possible, reloads should always be performed by using the appropriate QlikView services.

Obtaining QlikView software

QlikView software needs to be obtained by downloading it from the QlikTech web servers. To access the full set of downloads, you must be a registered user with an e-mail domain corresponding to a licensed customer.

Note that if you log in to the download site and see that the only download option is QlikView Desktop, this indicates that your credentials are not associated with a company that can download the QlikView software. (Usually, it automatically associates the credentials based on your e-mail address). Contact your partner or account manager to get the details updated on the server.

The URL for the downloading QlikView from the website is `http://www.qlikview.com/download`. This will redirect you to an appropriate download website close to the global region that you are in. For example, I am in Europe, so I will be redirected to `http://eu.demo.qlikview.com/download/`.

The download website is actually a QlikView application. On the left-hand side there are listboxes that allow you to drill down to the correct download option that you require. Once you have selected the correct version and service release, click on the link for the installer that matches your operating system. If I want to install the software on a 64-bit Windows 2008 Server, I will select `QlikViewServer_X64Setup.exe`.

If the last modified date is within the last couple of weeks, I would advise you to check the QlikView Community website (`community.qlikview.com`) to see if there are any known issues with the release. If there are known issues then it might be a better decision to install the previous service release.

I tend to download the **Server Reference Manual** and all of the QlikView Desktop Clients also. I will put these in a folder on the server called `QVInst`. This folder can be shared with appropriate users in order to allow them to install the client.

Confirming installation policies

You will need to check with the server administrators as to whether it is OK to go ahead and install QlikView in the default `Program Files` folder, or whether you need to install it on a separate drive.

You should note that the QlikView Server services will write configuration and logging files to the system's `ProgramData` folder (or `Documents and Settings\All Users\Application Data` on Windows 2003 or XP).

Some IT departments can be strict about applications writing files to the c: drive. If this is an issue, I recommend reviewing the options in *Barry Harmsen*'s blog post on the subject. Barry describes how to move the files to an alternate location (http://www.qlikfix.com/2013/08/15/moving-qlikview-server-log-files/).

Installing the QlikView Server step-by-step

The following steps can be performed by any user who has installation rights on the server. I recommend that for this step you to log in as the service account user. Logging in as the service account user will identify any issues, such as file access, that you might not discover until later if you use a different user. The service user should be a local administrator; so, you should have all the rights that are necessary to perform the installation.

1. Log in to the server as a user with installation rights. Remote Desktop is fine for this.

2. Locate the installer that you had downloaded earlier (for example, QlikViewServer_X64Setup.exe), and double-click on it to start the installation. The installation wizard is displayed, as shown in the following screenshot:

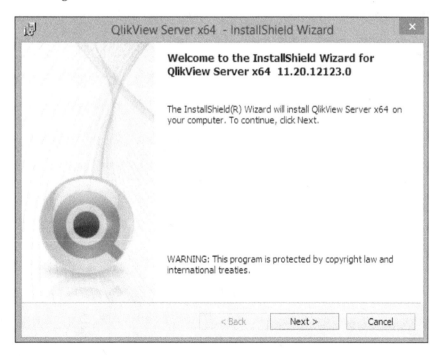

3. Click on **Next** to continue. On the next few screens, you will be asked to select your region, agree to the license agreement, and confirm your name and organization. Follow the prompts on these screens, until you get to the screen where you can confirm the installation folder, as follows:

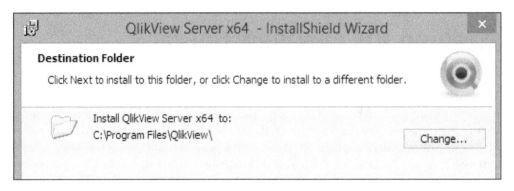

4. Select the correct path for the installation, as confirmed previously with the server administrators. Click on **Next** to continue:

5. There are several options, as shown in the preceding screenshot, for setting up the installation profile, which we will discuss in *Chapter 5, Installing QlikView Server Enterprise*. For now, select the default value—**Full Installation, Single machine with QlikView Webserver**. (Note that the IIS option is only available if IIS is installed on the server.) Click on **Next**:

6. At this stage, we can enter the login information for the service user, as shown in the preceding screenshot. If you don't have this information to hand right now, it can be entered manually in the Windows Services Management tool later on, and you can select the **I want to specify the account to be used for the services later.** checkbox. The **Browse** button allows you to browse domains and users. I tend to avoid this if possible, as it can be quite slow to scan. Once you have entered the required information, click on **Next**. The installer will validate the credentials and move on, if they are correct:

7. For this installation, we will use the default **Use QlikView Administrators Group** option, as shown in the preceding screenshot. Unless you have servers across different domains (refer to *Chapter 5, Installing QlikView Server Enterprise*), this option should always be used always. Click on **Next**.

8. In the **Ready to Install the Program** dialog box, you can go ahead and click on **Next** to start the installation:

9. After the installation is complete, note the important message about restarting the server. It is OK to go ahead and do another installation— for example, QlikView Desktop or the QlikView Offline Service—but you should reboot the server before moving on to configuring the QlikView Services. Click on **Finish** to close the dialog box.

10. Restart the server.

11. Once the server has been rebooted, log back in as the same user that you were logged in as at the time of installation. Open QlikView Management Console (we will look at QMC in more detail in the next chapter) from the **QlikView Program Group** or by opening an NTLM-enabled browser (IE and Chrome are NTLM-enabled browsers by default), and connect to the URL: `http://localhost:4780/QMC/default.htm`.

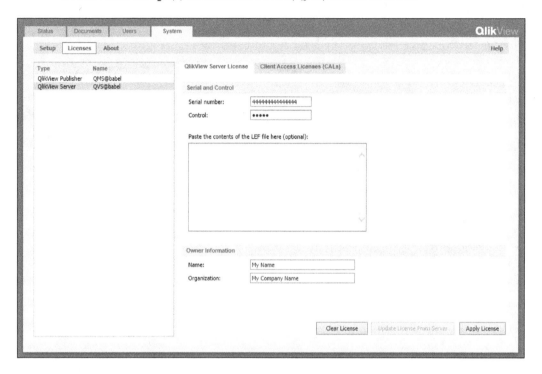

12. Click on the **System** tab and select **Licenses**. Select the **QlikView Server** license type, and then click on the **QlikView Server License** tab. Enter your serial number and control number (these will have been provided to you in a document from QlikTech, or from the QlikView Partner that you have purchased from). Enter the name and organization for the license owner. Click on **Apply License**.

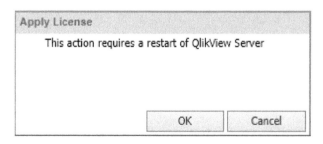

13. Click on **OK** in the message dialog box to restart QlikView Server, as shown in the preceding screenshot.

14. If all goes well, the **LEF (License Enabler File)** information will appear in the **Paste the contents of the LEF file here** area, and the word **Success** should appear just above the **Apply License** button. If things haven't gone correctly (perhaps because your server is not connected to the Internet or because of a firewall issue), you will need to obtain the LEF information from either your QlikView Partner or QlikTech directly. Once you have it, you can re-enter the license number, control number, name, and organization; paste the LEF information in the LEF area, and then click on **Apply License**. You will get the same restart message; click on **OK**. The license should apply correctly this time, as it doesn't need to go online.

 When pasting the LEF information, you should not have any leading or trailing spaces or carriage returns, as these may cause the application of the license to fail.

That's it. The server is now installed.

Testing the implementation

Testing the implementation is as simple as connecting to the AccessPoint website. First, on the server, use the localhost address: `http://localhost/qlikview/index.htm`.

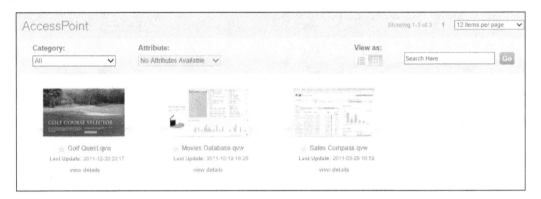

You could further test here by clicking on one of the demo documents.

 Note that, by default, the server will automatically assign you a named user license. You may not want to assign a license to this user at this time.

The next test is to ask one of your users to connect to the server at the server URL: `http://servername/qlikview/index.htm` or `http://servername.domain.com/qlikview/index.htm`.

Again, the user should be using an NTLM-enabled browser, and the server should fall under their local intranet profile; otherwise the authentication will not be automatically passed through. If they are not passed through, the user will be presented with a standard username/password dialog, which can be used to enter their credentials.

Summary

In this chapter, we looked at making sure that everything is in place for a QlikView installation. We looked at the requirements for our service account, installed Microsoft .NET Framework 4.0, and made sure that the correct connectivity drivers were in place. Then we downloaded the QlikView software from the download website. We then went ahead and worked through each step of installing QlikView Server. Finally, we tested the implementation.

In the next chapter, we will look at what has been installed, and will explore QlikView Management Console.

3
Exploring the QlikView Management Console in Detail

The **QlikView Management Console** (**QMC**) is the administrator's main portal into configuring and managing QlikView Server.

It is important to know what has been installed and where, so we will look at this. We will also talk about license management, mounting folders for QlikView documents, and other server settings.

These are the topics we'll be covering in this chapter:

- Looking at what has been installed
- Exploring the QlikView Management Console
- Licensing
- The Root and Mount folders
- Understanding other QlikView Server settings
- Customizing QlikView Web Server settings

Looking at what has been installed

Before we delve into the **QlikView Management Console (QMC)**, we are going to look at what has been installed and where they have been installed.

Some readers might think that this section should be placed towards the end of the previous chapter, and they may be right, but it is useful to set the context for the rest of the information that will be presented in this chapter:

Services

In the default installation that we performed in the previous chapter, there were five services installed. We can quickly verify this by running the standard Windows **Services** dialog, where we can see that each of them has been installed is set to **Automatic** start type, and has the correct login user.

 If you did not have the QlikView Service account details at the time of installation, or if you need to change the user details for some reason, you can change it using the Windows **Services** dialog window.

Name	Description	Status	Startup Type
QlikView Directory Service Connector	Keeps track ...	Running	Automatic
QlikView Distribution Service	The service ...	Running	Automatic
QlikView Management Service	Hosts the M...	Running	Automatic
QlikView Server	Hosts the Q...	Running	Automatic
QlikView Webserver	The web ser...	Running	Automatic

If you don't see the five services here, with each of them running, we need to do some troubleshooting.

The first step would probably be to assume that a wrong option was chosen during the installation, so we can uninstall (the easiest way is to just run the same installer .exe file again) and then re-install choosing the correct options. This option is always available to you as the settings (such as the license that we have entered) are retained, so we don't have to enter them again. To get a "clean" uninstall, we can uninstall and manually delete the ProgramData\QlikTech folder.

If the problem is just that one of the services hasn't started, it is a good idea to look at the Windows **Event** logs, and then at the logfile for the particular service (refer to the next section for folder information), which will usually point you to the right solution.

If we just can't work out what is going wrong, we should always remember the QlikView Community, where many issues have already been resolved, and we can post requests for help at `http://community.qlikview.com`.

Folders

During the installation process, we chose a `Program Files` folder (this defaults to `c:\ Program Files\QlikView`). This contains the EXE files for each of the services along with the supporting files for those executables, including some configuration files.

The main configuration files are stored in the program data folders, which will be created depending on the version of Windows server:

Windows Version	Path to program data folder
2003, XP	`C:\Documents and Settings\All Users\ Application Data\QlikTech`
2012, 2008, 7, Vista	`C:\ProgramData\QlikTech`

In this folder, you should find one file, `LEF.TXT`, and several subfolders. The `LEF` file contains the License Enablement information that was established when we added the server license, as explained in the previous chapter.

Each of these services will create its own subfolder. Within each of these subfolders, there will be files containing configuration information, as well as logging files and folders. Each service maintains a separate format and path for logging and settings. Luckily, we don't generally need to go and "hack" into these files—we can manage the services by using the Management Console.

The `Documents` folder is of interest because this is the default root folder for the QlikView server. If you look in here, you will see some QVW files, some PGO files, a QAR file, and a `README.TXT`. There may be some other associated files that we will discuss later.

The PGO files are the QlikView license files. Here, QlikView Server maintains details of who has been assigned licenses and of what type. These are binary files that you should *not* edit. These files are also replicated to the `QlikTech\QlikViewServer` folder.

The `QVW` files are the default demo documents, which you should have seen when you first opened the QlikView AccessPoint at the end of the previous chapter. Note that it is not a recommended configuration to have the QVW files in the root folder alongside your `PGO` files. Later, we will see how to reconfigure this.

Extensions

The QAR and README files are associated with each other, and are related to QlikView Extension Objects. These are HTML/XML/JavaScript files that can interact with QlikView data, and present new user interfaces that are not available out of the box with QlikView. For example, geographic mapping is a common use case.

Developers will create these objects on their own desktop PCs along with QlikView Desktop. To deploy them in QlikView Server, we need to create a `QlikTech\ QlikViewServer\Extensions\Objects` folder to contain them. Alternatively, they can be hosted elsewhere and we can configure QlikView Server to point at that alternate folder via the Management Console.

QlikView Management Console

As we saw in the previous chapter, the **QlikView Management Console (QMC)** is opened by going to the URL `http://servername:4780/QMC/default.htm`. If you are working on the server, then `localhost` can be used for the server name.

Only users who are members of the QlikView Administrators group on the server running the QlikView Management service have full access to the QMC. The user that was logged in while running the installation and the user name that was specified as the service user during the installation process will both be added to the QlikView Administrators group by default. Note that, if you are not logged into your PC (or the server or a Remote Desktop session) as one of those users, you will get an **Access Denied** message that tells you: **Membership of local security groups is missing**.

> Once you add yourself to the QlikView Administrators group, you may need to log off and log on again before the group configuration change becomes active and you can access QMC (this is a Windows feature, not a QlikView feature).

Licensing

All of your QlikView Server and Publisher licensing is managed via the QMC. In this section, we will look at managing our server license and license assignments.

Adding and updating licenses

We have already seen in the previous chapter how to add a new QlikView Server license by opening QMC by clicking on the **System** tab, then clicking on the **Licenses** button, selecting the QlikView Server (**QVS@servername**) from the list, and then selecting the **QlikView Server License** tab.

There are three buttons on this screen that are important to know about, which can be seen in the following screenshot:

The first button, **Clear License**, does exactly that. It will remove the QlikView Server license and leave the server in an unlicensed and unusable state. There is another side effect of this—all of your Named User license and Document license assignments will be removed. This can actually be a useful troubleshooting step, but you should record your license information before doing it (there is a useful Power Tool available from the QlikView Community that will help you do this— refer to *Chapter 8, Monitoring and Troubleshooting QlikView Server*). You will be prompted to restart the QlikView Server service after clearing the license.

When you buy new licenses for your server from QlikTech, you do not get a new server license number. You will get a new License document, and the licensing servers will be updated with the new details. At this point, you simply re-enter the **Control Number**, and click on the **Update License From Server** button. The QlikView licensing servers will be contacted and a new LEF file will be delivered, which contains the details of your new license configuration. This also requires restarting the QlikView Server service.

 It is worth noting that while the license number and current LEF information are displayed in the console, the control number is always cleared, so you will need to have it somewhere handy—a text file on the desktop may be a good choice.

Of course, you may have difficulty with this procedure because your server may not be connected to the internet, or you may have a firewall blocking the connection to the QlikView servers. In this case, you can obtain the text of the new LEF from either your QlikView partner or QlikTech directly. You can then enter the **Control Number**, paste the new LEF information over the old information, and then click the **Apply License** button. Again, you will be prompted to restart the QlikView Server service.

Managing client licenses

There are two types of user licenses that we can manage through the QMC, the Named User and the Document. Named User licenses are managed via the **Client Access Licenses (CALs)** tab of the **Licenses** screen. The Document licenses are managed at the document level via the main **Document** tab.

Licenses – General

The **General** screen of the **Client Access Licenses (CALs)** tab lists all of the different licenses that are assigned to the QlikView Server license.

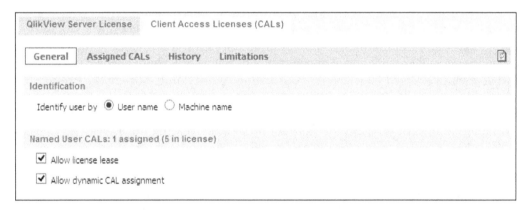

A license can be identified either by the username or by the machine name. This is a binary choice—you can use one or the other. The default is for the license to be identified by the user name. This makes sense when there is an increase in mobile-client users—these clients can only be identified by the user name, where the "thick" clients can only be identified by the machine name. In an organization where there are shared desktops, for example, a call center with shift workers, a machine name license scheme may be used with, say, the QlikView Plugin Client. It does require some thought, however, because it then excludes other client types.

The default option for Named User licenses is to allow them to be leased onto QlikView Desktop. This can be disabled here. However, if your users cannot lease a license, they will need to be given a separate license key for their QlikView Desktop.

 A user will actually be allowed to lease a license to two different machine IDs within one 24-hour period (for instance, their desktop and remote desktop session). Lease information is stored in the borrowedcal.pgo file on the server.

It is also the default option to allow licenses to be dynamically assigned — this means that if an unlicensed user connects to AccessPoint and tries to open a document (or performs an **Open in Server** operation from a QlikView Desktop), that user will be automatically assigned a Named User license, if there is one available. This can be useful but should be turned off if you have any other licenses in place, as Named User licenses will always be checked for first.

 When a user connects to a QlikView Server, the server goes through the different license types to check if that user has a license to access the document that they have tried to open. The order in which licenses are checked is: Named User license, Document license, Session license, and Usage license.

Managing Assigned users

Assigned users are those users who have been assigned a Named User license either automatically or manually. The **Assigned Users** screen of the **Client Access Licenses (CALs)** tab lists is shown in the following screenshot:

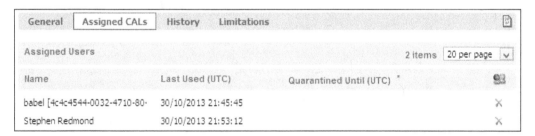

The list will either show usernames or machine names, not both, as they are mutually exclusive. If you have a license from another type left over after a change of options (as in the previous screenshot), or if you just need to remove a license from a user, you can click on the red **X** to the right of the user or machine name. You can delete several in one go by clicking on the **X** beside each one.

When you have completed removing the licenses, you need to click on the **Apply** button at the bottom of the screen. If you don't, then the license deletes will not apply.

QlikView will apply a 24-hour quarantine on any user who has used their license recently. If you try to delete it, it will not be freed up immediately, and a quarantine date and time will be shown:

Name	Last Used (UTC)	Quarantined Until (UTC)	
babel [4c4c4544-0032-4710-80·	30/10/2013 21:45:45	31/10/2013 21:45:45	

You can delete the license after the quarantine period, either manually or by restarting the QlikView Server.

We can add an assignment manually by clicking on the **Manage Users** icon on the right-hand side of the window:

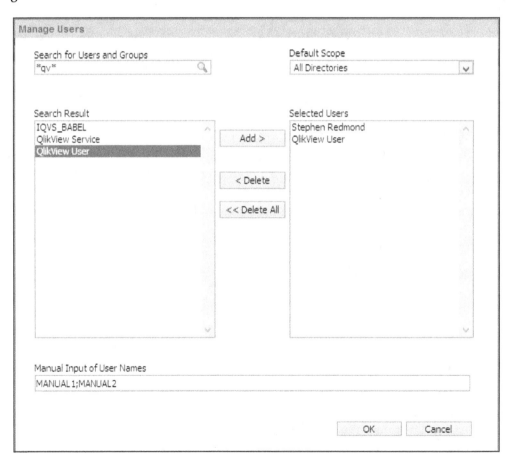

The search box allows you to search any of your directory service connectors (the default will be your Active Directory connection). You can search by using the full name (for example, QlikView User), username (for example, QVUser), domain and username (for example BABEL\QVUSER), or wildcard (where * replaces zero or more characters and ? replaces one character). In fact, you can combine all of these options into a semi colon-separated list of values, and all will be searched (this is useful if you have a long list of users that you want to add quickly).

There may be many reasons why you can't search your directory service for users or group at a particular time. You can always use the **Manual Input of User Names** option to enter the names in either DOMAIN\USER or just USER format, separated by a semicolon. Whether you use the DOMAIN bit or not is dependent on how the user will be identified to QlikView Server – the default would be via your Windows login, so it would be WINDOWSDOMAIN\USER. With custom users, you can use a DOMAIN\, which will identify the Directory Service Connector to use to resolve group membership (refer to *Chapter 7, Alternative Authentication and Authorization Methods*). You might have custom users that are not identified by the DOMAIN\ and that is fine if you don't need group resolution.

Once you have found users, you can select one or multiple (using the *Ctrl* key), and then click on the **Add** button to add them to the **Selected Users** list.

You also have the option to add a semicolon-separated list of usernames that are not in a directory service. This option would be used more often when using QlikView DMS security model instead of the default NTFS model.

Once you have clicked on **OK**, it is important to remember to click on the **Apply** button to save the user changes.

Managing Document licenses

Document licenses are managed at the document level.

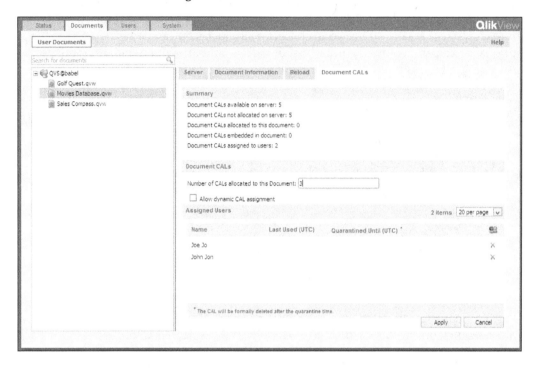

Click on the **Documents** tab, and open the list of documents under **User Documents**, and then click on the **Document CALs** tab. The **Summary** tells you how many Document licenses are available and how many have been assigned. You can enter the number of licenses to allocate to this document. Assigned users are added in the same way as named users—either by allowing automatic assignment or by manually assignment via the **Manage Users** button.

You must click on the **Apply** button to save any changes that you make.

Remember that you should remove all of the document licenses from a document before you remove that document from the server. If you don't, these licenses can become **orphaned**— unassigned but unavailable to assign to another document. Further details on this are given later.

Also, it is worth noting that you can make changes on any of the tabs of the document properties before you need to click on the **Apply** button. However, it is probably a good idea to click it for each tab.

The Root and Mount folders

As mentioned previously, it is not recommended to have QVW files published in the same folder as the PGO files that contain the license information. There is no technical reason for this; it is really a matter of best practice. One can often add and remove QVW and other files from the server folders—we wouldn't want to accidentally remove or somehow overwrite a PGO file. By separating the root folder and the application folders, we reduce the possibility of anything going awry.

The QVS folder structure

It is not critical to follow the instructions given. What is critical is that you do follow some sort of standard for your implementation. There are other frameworks available. My belief is that the following recommendations are easy to follow and logical in their implementation.

On most servers, you will not use the C: drive to store your documents. Most probably, an administrator will have created a partition for your files. Even if you are using the C: drive, it is not recommended to use the default ProgramFiles folder structure that QlikView creates during the default installation.

As mentioned earlier, it is a matter of good practice, and in CapricornVentis we recommend to use a folder structure that separates the server root folder (containing the PGO files) and the user applications. We like to create a folder structure based on business area, for example, Finance, Sales, HR, and so on, or based on whatever is right for the business we are working with.

We might have a folder structure like this:

In this case, the Root folder is separated from the application files, which helps to avoid accidental interference with the PGO files.

The subfolders under each of the departmental folders will be the same for each department. Any of these folders may have appropriate subfolders.

As mentioned earlier, this is not the only way that you could structure this; it is just one way. Other frameworks might create many more folders. The most important thing is to follow a structure.

The main folders are:

Folder name	Use
Sources	This folder contains source table files (Excel, XML, CSV, and so on) It will often be shared to a person responsible for updating and maintaining the data.
Loader	This folder contains QVW files that have the sole purpose of connecting to data sources and generating QVD files.
QVD	This folder contains the QVD files generated by the loaders.
UserApp	This folder contains the final QVW files that will be presented on AccessPoint.

This folder structure would be for a QlikView Server with no Publisher. When Publisher is used, this structure would be on the Publisher Server. Only the UserApp folder would be on the QlikView Server.

Create the new Root and Mount folders

In the QMC, we need to go to the **System** tab and look at the **Setup** screen. Open the QlikView Servers and select the server (**QVS@servername**). Click on the server's **Folders** tab.

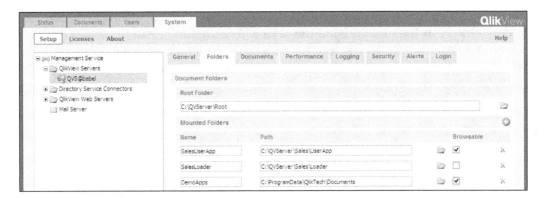

Change the path of the Root Folder to the newly created folder. Click on the + button to add the newly mounted folders. Give each a name and a valid path. Note that if the contents of a folder should not be visible to users in the AccessPoint, as for loader documents, you should clear the **Browsable** checkbox.

As mentioned earlier, you wouldn't mount Loader folders on the server when using Publisher; only the UserApp folders will be mounted.

Be careful when entering multiple folders if you are manually typing the folder paths. If the path is invalid then the entry will not be accepted. In fact, if you enter one invalid path along with several correct ones, they will all be rejected. It is advisable to click on **Apply** often.

Also, note that the **Browsable** option did have a problem in some older versions of QlikView, where the contents were displayed to the users—this has been fixed in the more recent versions. You also need to ensure that the **Respect browsable flag on mount** option is set to on (which is the default), within the QlikView Web Server settings. I can't think of a reason not to have this option on!

As always, we must click on **Apply** for this setting to be applied. Whenever the root folder changes, the server will need to be restarted and you will be prompted to do so.

Licenses gotcha!

In this case, we have moved the location of the root folder and when QlikView Server restarts, it will move the PGO files into that folder and all will be clean. However, we have an issue here.

Earlier, we configured Document licenses for one of the documents in the demo folder, which was the root folder at the time. This assignment will remain in the server PGO files, but the file no longer exists! This is something that can happen with both license assignments and reload schedules if folders are moved or if a QVW document is renamed.

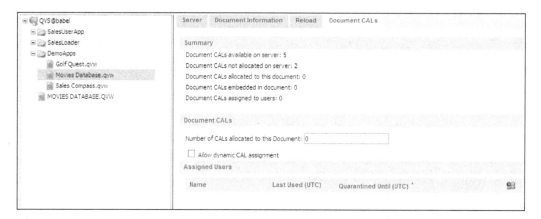

In this case, we can see that even though three Document licenses have been assigned on the server, they are no longer assigned to the Movies Database file. Additionally, there is a "ghost" document listed, **MOVIES DATABASE.QVW**, with its title all in capitals.

There are a couple of ways to resolve this issue. We have already discussed clearing the server license, which will remove all license assignments. This is the so called "nuclear" option. The easiest way to resolve it is to not let it happen! Remove license assignments from documents before you move folders or rename them.

There is a simple fix here. If we create a QVW file in the root folder with the same name as the original (it doesn't have to bear any resemblance to the original, just the name), then QMC will allow us to remove the licenses. Once you have cleared the licenses, you can simply delete the dummy file. This is a useful trick to know about—it works for licenses and for reload schedules.

Understanding other QlikView Server settings

Within the QMC, there are many settings that you may never change, but they are still useful to know about.

Alternate extensions path

We discussed extension objects earlier in this chapter. If you need to specify an alternate path to extension objects, you can do so on the same **Folders** tab where we changed the root folder earlier.

You can also define the folder that QlikView will use to create temporary files (images, PDFs, and so on here).

Session collaboration

Session collaboration is a feature of QlikView 11.x that allows users to share their sessions with other people — whether those people have a license or not. Everyone can view the same screen and make selections, which changes the view for everyone.

To allow session collaboration, you must first turn it on. This is done by selecting a checkbox on the **Documents** tab of the **Server** settings called Allow Session Collaboration.

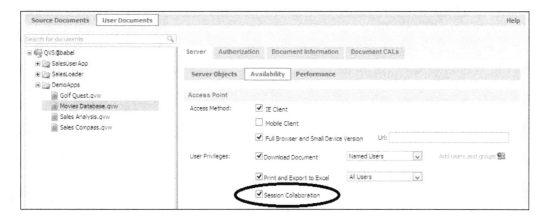

On a document-by-document basis, you can then turn on **Session Collaboration** under the document's **Server** tab, under **Availability**.

Logging

There are several different logging options for QlikView Server.

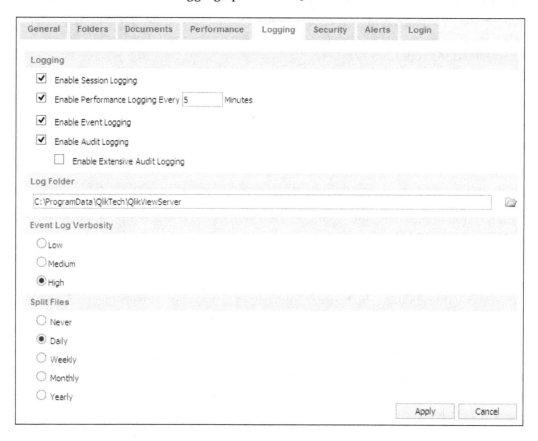

We talk more about logfiles in *Chapter 8, Monitoring and Troubleshooting QlikView Server*, but it is worth mentioning the **Split Files** option here. It is set to **Never** by default, which will create one large logfile. It is useful to change this so as to have a smaller set of files. The **Daily** option, for example, will create a new logfile every day. Having multiple files makes it easier to archive older files as part of routine server maintenance.

The different log types are:

Log type	Details
Session	All user sessions are logged, which includes details such as the name of user, connection time, disconnection time, documents opened, and so on.
Performance	Server-level information such as number of sessions, memory statistics, among others logged, by default, every 5 minutes.
Event	Event logs record server-level information and error messages that are also logged to the Windows event logs. It records license use, documents loading into memory, system errors, and so on.
Audit	This will log much more detail about a user's session — what they clicked on, the selections they made, sheets they opened, bookmarks that were applied, and so on.
Extensive audit	This goes into even more detail than the audit option. For example, when applying a bookmark, it will record the selections in the bookmark.

 Be warned, if the auditing process is on, performance could potentially suffer.

Security

For most installations, the default security options will be applied. These will need to change if you are not using Active Directory but are using an alternative authentication method (refer to *Chapter 7, Alternative Authentication and Authorization Methods*).

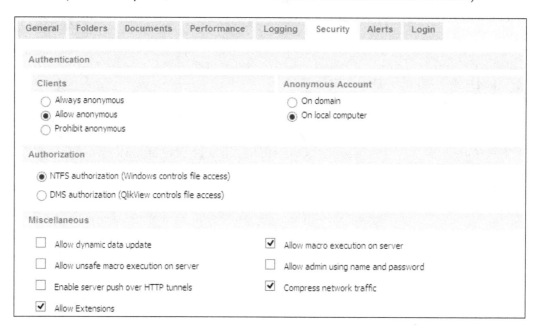

The **Allow anonymous** option is linked to a user called IQVS_servername that is generated when QlikView Server first starts. Depending on the server type, this is either a local account or a domain account. If you want to have anonymous users (which will only work with Concurrent licenses or on a QlikView Information Access Server), the IQVS_user will need to be granted access to those QVW files.

The **Authorization** option controls how QlikView behaves once a user has been authenticated elsewhere. By default, it will accept Windows authentication, and use the NTFS security on the files and folders to grant users access to the files via AccessPoint. If DMS is selected, then you need to assign users and groups to each of the documents using QMC. We will look at this in more detail in the next chapter.

Alerts

The **Alerts** option allows us to specify some e-mail addresses that will be used to alert administrators when reloads fail. For this to work, you need to configure the **Mail Server** under **Setup**.

Management Service settings

The Management Service is the service that pulls everything together. It controls all of the central settings, all of the reload schedules, and manages the QlikView Management Console itself.

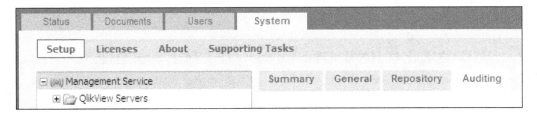

To manage the Management Service settings, we need to click on **Management Service** — the root node — on the **Setup** screen.

The General tab

The **Summary** tab doesn't have any settings. It does contain the URL for the management service, which is `http://servername:4799/QMS/Service`.

This is the address, needed by external applications, that will make calls to the Management Service **API (Application Programming Interface)**.

This address is also displayed (twice!) on the **General** tab.

The main setting on the **General** tab is the **Logging Level**, which can be **No logging**, **Normal logging**, or **Debug logging**.

The Repository tab

The Repository is where the Management Service keeps its settings. By default, this is in a folder containing XML files. The default name is **QVPR (QlikView Publisher Repository)**.

As we have seen in the previous chapter, this tab can be used to change where the repository is stored to be an SQL Server database.

If you are keeping the XML format (and in most circumstances it is fine to do so), you can schedule how often the XML files are zipped to backup files — it is up to you to arrange a backup of these files to a safe storage location.

The Auditing tab

QlikView allows the changes that are made by administrators in the QlikView Management Console to be logged. This option is not turned on by default.

The **Auditing** tab allows you to turn on this auditing of the QMC. It also allows you to specify the location of the logfiles.

Customize QlikView Web Server settings

QlikView Web Server is a self-contained, fully functional web server that does not rely on Microsoft IIS to deliver web content to users.

In most circumstances, especially with the default installation as we have done in the previous chapter, we don't need to worry about these settings too much as it tends to just work. However, it is useful to know about these settings so that you can make changes if necessary.

The General tab

The **General** tab allows us to specify general options for the web server.

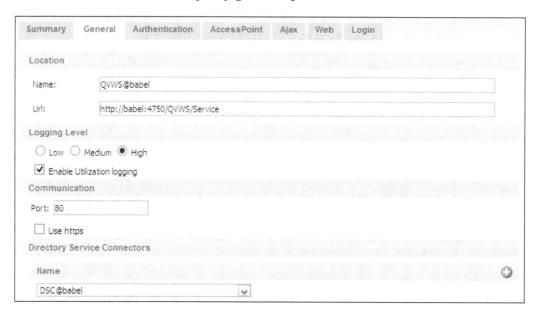

Usually, the **Name** and **Url** under **Location** will not need to be changed, but if you change the name of your server, you will need to change them here.

The **Logging Level** is similar to what we have seen before. The **High** setting will record the most information. We also have the option to **Enable Utilization logging**, which will record some additional statistics about the server when opening documents.

The communication settings allow us to define the port and SSL usage for the web server.

> To enable SSL for an IIS based system is relatively straightforward, but not so easy for a QlikView Web Server. Obtaining a certificate for a computer is relatively straightforward (refer to http://technet.microsoft.com/en-us/library/bb727068.aspx for information on obtaining a computer certificate). Once the certificate is in place, you can bind it to the SSL port by following the instructions at http://msdn.microsoft.com/en-us/library/ms733791.aspx.
>
> Once that is configured, you can set the **Port** option for the web server to 443 (the default port for secure traffic) and set the **Use https** option on.

Finally, the **Directory Service Connectors** setting tells the QVWS where to connect to for user-group resolution (refer to *Chapter 7, Alternative Authentication and Authorization Methods*, for more information).

The Authentication tab

This tab allows us to specify how users will be authenticated to this QlikView Web Server.

We will discuss the settings on this tab in detail in *Chapter 7, Alternative Authentication and Authorization Methods*.

The AccessPoint tab

The **AccessPoint** tab controls settings for the QlikView portal that users will use to access their documents.

There are two subtabs on this tab.

AccessPoint settings

The following screenshot shows the tab that affects the defaults for the AccessPoint that users will see:

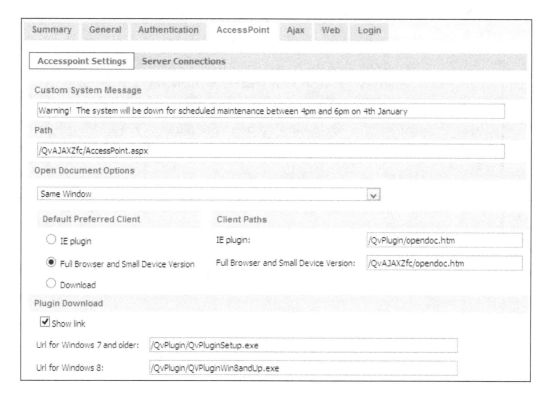

The **Custom System Message** option allows you to add a message that will appear at the top of the AccessPoint when the user logs in. It can be used for any purpose that you wish.

The **Path** option allows you to point to a customized `AccessPoint.aspx` file.

> Maintaining customizations in a different file means that you can be sure that they won't be overwritten by any upgrade. Note that, in this case and others, the path can be customized but the name of the aspx file must be the same. This is a security feature of QlikView Server, in that it will only serve known filenames.

There are a number of options under the **Open Document Options** settings. The first allows you to specify how documents will open when a user clicks on them in AccessPoint. The default is to open the documents in the same window. You can choose to open them in a new window or re-use an existing open window.

The **Default Preferred Client** setting specifies the client that will be used by default when a user clicks on a document in AccessPoint. The user has the option to define their own default under **Favorites & Profile** in AccessPoint.

The **Client Paths** setting defines the URLs that the system uses to open a document. You can create customized versions of these files to add your own functionality (which could be related, for example, to security). The path is customized but the filenames must remain the same.

Finally, the **Plugin Download** option specifies whether the **Download Internet Explorer Plugin** option displays to the user in AccessPoint. As of SR4 of version 11.2, this option should detect the Windows version, and download the appropriate one for the user.

Server Connections

The **Server Connections** option allows us to specify what QlikView Server this web server will connect to, and how to handle clusters.

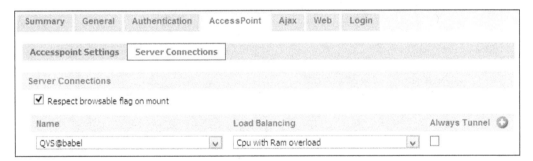

I can't think of a good reason why you would not want to have the **Respect browsable flag on mount** option selected. If this is off, the flag set against folder mounts will be ignored.

The **Name** option allows you to define the QlikView Server to connect to.

We will see in *Chapter 5, Installing QlikView Server Enterprise*, that QlikView Servers in a cluster are referred to under the same name, which will be **QVS@first_server_added**. We don't need to worry about that here; we just need to specify the **Load Balancing** option. There are three options:

Option	Description
Cpu with Ram overload	This option has the web server request load information from the QlikView Servers in the cluster. The web server will direct the user to a server that can deliver the best results to the user.
Loaded document	The web server interrogates the QlikView Servers in the cluster to see if the requested document has already been loaded in one of them. If it is, it will direct the user to that server.
Random	The user will be connected to a server based on a random selection.

The Ajax tab

This tab has a few interesting options regarding how the web server works — not necessarily to do with Ajax!

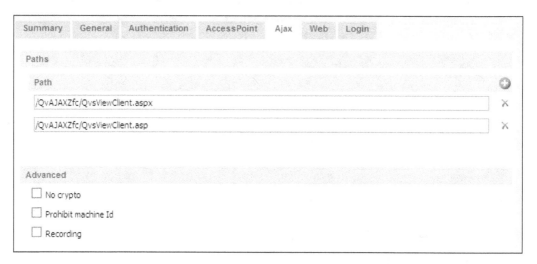

Again, we have some options to specify custom options on the path to the QvsViewClient.aspx. However, the name of the file must not be changed.

The **No Crypto** option turns off the securely encrypted communication between the QlikView Server and the web server. It is not really recommended to turn this off in any circumstances — it should not be turned off on a public web server. If you have anonymous users, they may be allowed to create bookmarks. As they are anonymous, the bookmarks are stored against their machine ID instead. If you choose to **Prohibit machine Id**, those users will not be able to create bookmarks.

The **Recording** option will start creating a file, by default, in the `C:\ProgramData\QlikTech\WebServer` folder called `Recording.log`. This will contain a record of all the **QVPX (QlikView Protocol)** XML data passed between the web server and the QlikView Server.

The Web tab

The **Web** tab allows you to mention the Web-specific items that this web server will handle.

This includes default **Mime Types** and **Folders**. It is possible to add additional folders here — such as ones to hold customized content.

One thing that I quite often do, especially if this web server is dedicated to QlikView, is to add a new **Root Folder** with a blank **Name**, pointing to the same **Path** as the **QLIKVIEW** entry (defaults to C:\Program Files\QlikView\Web). This has the effect that users can just enter http://yourservername and it will open AccessPoint.

Summary

In this chapter, we looked at more details about the QlikView Management Console. We explored the folder structures that QlikView created when a server was installed and the services themselves. We used QlikView Management Console to add, remove, and update licenses, and we managed how those licenses were assigned to users. We reconfigured our folder structure to a better practice model, and we explored some of the other QlikView server settings, such as logging, security, and alerts.

In the next chapter we will look in more detail at managing and securing documents, and look at how to configure reloads on a standard QlikView Server.

4

Managing and Securing QlikView Documents

The role of a QlikView Server is to serve QlikView Documents to users. Of course, you will probably not want all of your documents served to all users, so you will need a way to secure your system.

In addition to document security, there are other server-side settings that are important to know for both server performance and user experience. We also need to know how to perform an automated reload if we don't have a QlikView Publisher in place. These are the topics we'll be covering in this chapter:

- Securing QlikView Documents
    - ° By license
    - ° Section Access
    - ° NTFS **Access Control List (ACL)**
    - ° QlikView **Document Metadata Service (DMS)**
- Other Document properties
    - ° Document Server settings
    - ° Document metadata
    - ° QlikView Server reload tasks
- Using **Event Driven Execution (EDX)**

Securing QlikView Documents

Making documents available to the correct users can be handled in several different ways, depending on your implementation and license structure. These methods are not mutually exclusive and you may choose to implement a combination of them.

By license

If you only have named Document users, you can restrict access to documents by simply not granting users a license. If users do not have a Document license for a particular document, they may be able to see that document in AccessPoint, but will not be able to open it.

You will need to turn off any automatic allocation of licenses for both Document licenses and Named User licenses, or the system will simply override your security by allocating an available license and giving the user access to that document.

This only works for Document license users. The Named User license holders can't be locked out of a document this way as they have a license that allows them to open any number of documents, so they cannot be restricted. The fact that this is user based — a Document license can only be granted to a user, not a group — also means that there is no option to secure by a named group.

This is the most basic, least flexible, and least user-friendly way to implement security. While it will certainly stop users getting access to documents — and it will work in either NTFS or DMS security modes — it can be frustrating for users to see a document that they think can open, but for which they will get a **NO CAL** error when they try to open it.

The QlikView file will also need to have appropriate NTFS or DMS security (refer to the next sections) so that users would be able to access it. The easiest way to do this is to grant access to a group that all the users will be in, or even allow access to an Authenticated Users group.

Section Access

Section Access security is a very effective way of securing a document to the correct set of users. This is because a user must be actually listed in the Section Access user list for the document to be even listed in AccessPoint for them.

Additionally, if Section Access is in place, a user cannot even connect by using a direct access URL because they have no security access to the data.

This method of securing documents works well in both NTFS and DMS security modes.

 When using the NTLM (Windows authentication via Internet Explorer) authentication method, you can have Group Names listed in Section Access. However, when using alternative authentication (refer to *Chapter 7, Alternative Authentication and Authorization Methods*), Section Access does not give us an option to secure by group.

As with the license method discussed earlier, appropriate file security needs to be in place in order to allow all the users access the QlikView file.

For more information on implementing Section Access, please refer to *QlikView 11 for Developers* by *Barry Harmsen* and *Miguel Garcia*, and *QlikView for Developers Cookbook* by *Stephen Redmond*, both published by *Packt Publishing*.

NTFS Access Control List (ACL)

NTFS (Microsoft's NT File System) security is the default method of securing access to files in a QlikView implementation. It works very well for installations where all the users are Windows users within the same domain or a set of trusted domains.

In NTFS security mode, the **Access Control List** (**ACL**) of the QlikView file is used to list the documents for a particular user. This is a very straightforward way of securing access and will be very familiar to Windows system administrators.

As with normal Windows file security, the security can be applied at the folder level. Windows security groups can also be used. Between groups and folder security, very flexible levels of security can be applied.

By default, Internet Explorer and Google Chrome will pass through the Kerberos/NTLM credentials to sites in the local Intranet zone. For other browsers, such as Safari on the iPad, the user will be prompted for a username and password. When a user connects to AccessPoint and their credentials are established, they are compared against the ACLs for all the files hosted by QVS. Only those files that the user has access to—either directly by name or by group membership—will be listed in AccessPoint.

Document Metadata Service (DMS)

For non-Windows users, QlikView provides a way of managing user access to files called the **Document Metadata Service (DMS)**. We will look at alternative authentication methods in *Chapter 7, Alternative Authentication and Authorization Methods*.

DMS uses a `.META` file in the same folder as the `.QVW` file to store the Access Control List. The Windows ACL, which has permissions on the file, now becomes mostly irrelevant as it is not used to authenticate users. It is only the QlikView service account that will need access to the file.

It is a binary choice between using NTFS or DMS security on any one QlikView Server.

Enabling DMS

To enable DMS, we need to make a change to the server configuration.

In the QlikView Management Console, on the **Security** tab of the QVS settings screen, we change **Authorization** to **DMS authorization** and then click on the **Apply** button.

The QlikView Server service will need to be restarted for this change to take effect. Once the service has restarted, a new tab, **Authorization**, becomes available in the document properties:

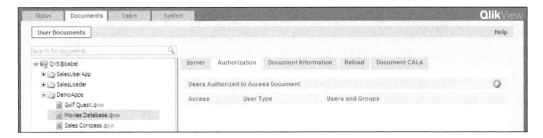

Clicking on the **+** button to the right of this tab allows you to enter new details of **Access**, **User Type**, and specific **Users and Groups**.

Access is either set to **Always** or **Restricted**. When **Access** is set to **Always**, the associated user or group will have access at any time. If it is set to **Restricted**, you can specify a time range and specific days when the user or group has access.

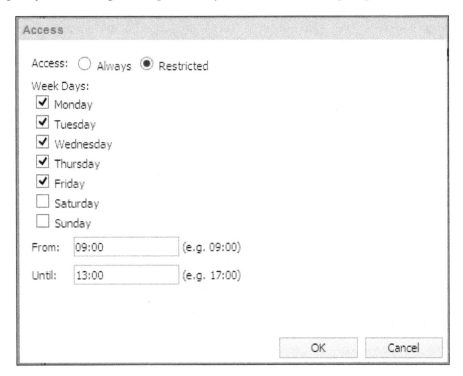

You can keep clicking on the + button to add as many sets of restricted times as needed for a user or group. The restrictions are additive; that is, if the user only has access on Monday and Tuesday in one group of restrictions, and then Thursday and Friday in another set of restrictions, they will therefore, have access on all four days.

The **User Type** is one of the following categories:

User Type	Details
All Users	Essentially no security. Any user, including anonymous, who can access the server will be able to access the file.
All Authenticated Users	For most implementations, this will also be **All Users**. However, it will not give access to anonymous users. The Section Access would typically be used to manage the security.
Named Users	This allows you to specify a list of named users and/or groups that will have specific access to the document.

If **Named Users** is selected, a **Manage Users** button will appear that allows you to specify users and/or groups in exactly the same way as we managed users for licenses in the previous chapter (refer to *Chapter 3, Exploring the QlikView Management Console in Detail*).

Other Document properties

Up to this point, we have looked at Document license administration and Document authorization. Now we will look at the other tabs that make up the Document properties in QMC.

Document Server settings

The Document **Server** settings tab defines how the document interacts with QlikView Server and users on the server:

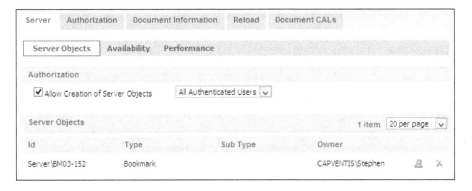

Server Objects (collaboration)

Collaboration is the facility in QlikView Server that allows users to create their own content, such as list boxes, charts, and so on.

Collaboration can be turned off globally for all Server documents in the **System** | **QVS settings** | **Documents** tab, by deselecting the **Allow Server Objects** option.

On a document-by-document basis, you can also turn it on for **All Authenticated Users** or **Named Users**. The named users are managed by the same dialog that we used to read details from the DSC.

We can also use this screen to view the list of objects that have been created by different users, and remove them if required (a valuable troubleshooting step). You should see that every user that has opened a document will have at least one bookmark. This bookmark is used for the **Session Recovery** function of QlikView Server, where a user's session is maintained if the user is disconnected.

Availability

Under availability, you can define the Access Method by which a particular document can be opened from AccessPoint. The defaults are IE client (plugin), Full Browser, and Small Device Version (AjaxZfc). You can also add the mobile client, but you should note that this is not the newest iPad application that uses Ajax, but the old clients such as the Java client for BlackBerry.

We can also define **User Privileges**, which are **Download Document** and **Print and Export to Excel**. These privileges can also be linked to either **All Users**, **All Authenticated Users**, or **Named Users**.

The final privilege is **Session Collaboration**, which is either on or off per document — not per user. This feature allows users to share one QlikView AjazZfc session with many other users, for shared discovery.

> The **Session Collaboration** feature was introduced in Version 11 of QlikView. It allows users to share their QlikView session with other users. They share a link (via e-mail, instant message, and so on) and every collaborating user sees the same screen; every user can make selections and change tabs (which can be potentially confusing!).

All of these privileges may either be enabled or disabled globally in the **Documents** tab of the QVS settings.

Performance

The performance option allows you to control how the document will behave when it is loaded and users are connecting.

We can control a number of session settings at the document level that override the server's default settings (set in the QVS settings' **Performance** and **Logging** tabs):

Setting	Description	Server Default
Maximum Number of Concurrent Sessions	This is the maximum number of sessions that will be allowed on this one document. Typically, this might be used with a very large document that consumes a lot of user cache memory. By restricting the number of user sessions, we can leave memory available for other documents, or just prevent the server from crashing!	5,000
Maximum Inactive Session Time	The time after which an unused session is considered to have ended. You can set this to 0 to indicate no session timeout—useful for an application used in a factory floor on a large screen where there is no interaction.	1,800 seconds (30 minutes)
Document Timeout	The time after which an unused document will be removed from memory. It can be used to free up resources from a large, unused document but should be weighed against the time taken to reload that document later. It can be set this to a small value where you have many small documents—the time taken to reload will be small in comparison with having the memory freed up.	Not documented but I believe it to be 480 minutes.

Setting	Description	Server Default
Enable Audit Logging	Audit logging needs to be enabled at the QVS level first, but you can then disable at each document level.	On

We can also specify the **Document Control** options here, which dictate how the document behaves in a clustered environment and whether the document should always be preloaded into memory.

When we have multiple QlikView servers configured in a cluster, the usual option is that the document is available **Always on All Nodes**. You can also specify a custom option—for example, the document is only available on one of the nodes, or that it will be available on all nodes but only preloaded into memory on one specific node.

The **Preload** option will make sure that the document is always loaded into memory (which overrides the **Document Timeout** settings).

> The load into memory happens every time the document is reloaded. It is worth noting that even when the document is preloaded into memory, only the core data for that document is loaded, and it may still take a moment to establish the baseline user cache when the first user connects.

Document metadata

The **Document Information** tab allows us to specify metadata about this document. Some of this metadata is displayed to users and some is used for internal functions.

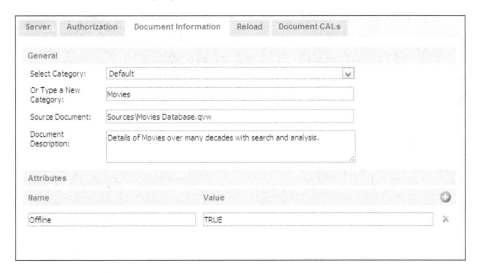

The **Select Category** field, which defaults to a value of **Default**, is searchable by users in the AccessPoint. It is also used to display the document's reload status in QMC.

The **Document Description** field is a free text field that allows you to specify information about the document that the users can view in AccessPoint.

The **Attributes** property can be totally arbitrary and is searchable in AccessPoint. It can also be used to serve other functions, such as enabling offline functionality in the QlikView iPad client.

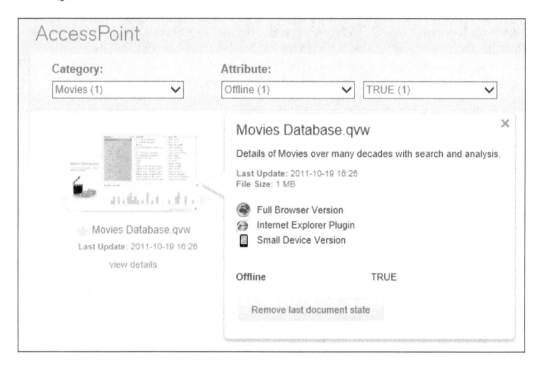

The user will see any description information that you enter, clients that the document can be opened with, and any attribute displayed in a pop-up window when they click on the **view details** link in AccessPoint.

QlikView Server reload tasks

Without a Publisher license, we can still configure and run one reload task per document on the QlikView Server. The following triggers can be configured for this reload task:

Trigger	Description
Hourly	Not strictly hourly, this will execute every x hours and y minutes. It could be every 1 minute.
Daily	The task is triggered every day at the specified time.
Weekly	The task is triggered once per week on the specified day at the specified time.
Monthly	The task is triggered once per month on the specified day of the month (1 to 31 or "Last Day") at the specified time.
Continuously	The task runs, completes, then runs again, repeatedly. This could potentially affect server resources.
On Event from Another Task	Whether another task is successful or has failed, this task kicks off. This allows us to chain multiple tasks together.
On an External Event	**Event Driven Execution, EDX** (refer to the next section).

There are some other settings that are not related to the triggers:

Setting	Description
Timeout seconds	The time before a reload task is considered to have timed out and hence failed.
Dependency	Allows you to specify one other task that must have completed successfully on its last attempt before this task will be allowed to trigger.
Data Protection	If your document is accessed by QlikView users with Section Access (rather than specifying the QlikView service user under NTNAME), you can specify the credentials to open the document here. That user must have reload rights.

Once a task has been scheduled, it will display in the **Tasks** section of the **Status** tab in QMC.

The logs for the reload job will be created in a subfolder of `ProgramData\QlikTech\DistributionService` — usually a folder called **1**. There is a separate subfolder created in the logs folder for each day. Within this, there is a separate folder created for each reload-triggered event.

This folder contains the task logfile, which is viewable in QMC by clicking on **Show Task Details**. If you have the **Generate Logfile** option turned on in the **Document Properties** of the `QVW` file (which I strongly recommend), a copy of that logfile will also be kept in this subfolder.

Using Event Driven Execution (EDX)

We have seen in the previous section that we can use the QlikView Server to schedule reloads on different kinds of triggers. Without having QlikView Publisher, we can only have one trigger per reload. This is generally enough for most purposes, but some organizations may have a requirement for more flexible reload schedules.

One of the triggers, **Event Driven Execution (EDX)**, is not time based. This trigger allows a web service call to be made to the QlikView Management Service (Service wsdl is `http://servername:4799/QMS/Service`) to start the task. A password can also be specified here. This allows external applications to trigger your QlikView reloads.

Not all of us are developers who can run an application to make web service calls. Luckily, someone has created a command-line executable and made this available for free download from the QlikView Community at `http://community.qlikview.com/docs/DOC-2650`.

For those who like taking things apart to see how it works, you can also look at the code on the GitHub page of *Rikard Brathen* at `https://github.com/braathen`.

Using the executable will allow us to trigger the execution of EDX tasks from a batch file, which can then be executed by the Windows scheduler, or indeed, any third-party scheduler.

The command line can be as simple as:

```
QMSEDX.exe -task="Sales Analysis.qvw" -pwd=mypassword
```

In this example, I am calling the EDX task associated with the Sales Analysis document. With QlikView Server, there can only be one trigger per document, so the task name is the same as the document name. If you are using EDX with QlikView Publisher, you can have multiple tasks per document, so you can specify the name of the task.

There are several other parameters, such as being able to specify the connection to the QMS, and a description for these can be found by just running the executable with no parameters.

Another scenario for running an EDX task is that a particular user needs to update some data before the QlikView document reloads. For example, they may need to close a period in the accounts system, or update a forecast in an Excel worksheet. For this to work, the user who runs the task must be a member of either the QlikView Administrators group on the QlikView Server. If you don't want the users to be able to access the QMC, you can alternatively create a Windows user group on the QlikView Server called `QlikView EDX`, and add the users to this.

Summary

In this chapter, we have looked at several ways of securing QlikView Documents — by license, using Section Access, utilizing NTFS ACLs, and implementing QlikView's DMS authorization. We have also looked at other Document properties such as Server settings, Document metadata, and how to configure a QlikView Server reload task. We have also discussed how EDX works and how it can be implemented.

In the next chapter, we will see how to implement QlikView in an Enterprise situation by installing QlikView Server components on separate servers.

5
Installing QlikView Server Enterprise

QlikView has spread extensively into enterprise accounts over the last several years. To serve large applications and a large user population, one server with all of the services running on it will not be sufficient. Therefore, we need to think about deploying services on different servers.

In a multiserver environment, QlikView Server should sit on its own server to give it maximum access to the hardware resources, without having to share those resources with other services.

For resilience, QlikView Server can be deployed on several servers with a shared document store and shared licenses. In the default configuration for a cluster, the QlikView Web Server service can query the QlikView servers for resource-load information and make the intelligent choice as to which QlikView Server in the cluster will serve the document to an user. If one of the servers in the cluster goes down, the other servers will pick up its load.

The demonstration in this chapter will cover the installation of different services across four different servers in the QVTRAINING domain, and one standalone Web server; the role of each server is given in the following table:

Server	Role
Server1	This hosts QlikView Management Service and Directory Service Connector. Also, this server will host the shared folders for the QlikView Server cluster.
Server2	This is the first server in a two-server cluster.
Server3	This is the second server in the cluster.
Server4	This hosts Publisher/QlikView Distribution Service.
Server5	This is a QlikView Web server running on **Internet Information Services** (**IIS**). This is a standalone server with IIS already installed.

Because our (fictitious) company policy states that any web servers should be on nondomain servers, this means we can't rely on the QlikView Administrators group for authentication between services. Therefore, we will deploy authentication with certificates instead of the QlikView Administrators group.

The default installation uses the QlikView Administrators group to authenticate the communication between services. The use of certificates allow the servers to be authorized to communicate with the server running the **QlikView Management Service** (**QMS**) that is acting as the certificate authority.

The requirements in the *Preparing the QlikView Environment* section in *Chapter 2, Standard Installation Process*, of having .NET Framework 4.0 and a service account user configured will still apply. Even though the service account user is not used as part of the authentication of the service communication, the account will still need rights to access files and folders.

The requirement to ensure that the connection software is in place is only necessary for the Publisher server, as that is the only box that will be performing reloads.

Also, it is worth noting that the certificates option is only available on Windows Server 2008 and later.

The first server that must be installed is the server that will run the QMSs. We will also establish a Windows shared folder on this server to store our QlikView documents and license files for the servers in the cluster.

> There is no particular reason for the choice of establishing the shared folder on the QMS server. It can be established on any Windows Server — but it must be a Windows Server! The shares that are established directly on **Network-attached storage** (**NAS**) or Storage area network (**SAN**) devices are not supported by QlikView and may cause file corruption. You can still use a SAN or NAS, but it must be mounted as a drive on a Windows Server, and then the folders can be shared.

These are the topics we'll be covering in this chapter:

- Installing the QMS and DSC service
- Testing the services installation
- Establishing the shared folder
- Creating the Publisher folders
- Installing the QVS service
- Testing the QVS installation
- Installing the QDS (Publisher) service
- Testing the QDS installation
- Installing the QlikView Web Service in IIS
- Testing the web installation
- Connecting servers to QMS

Installing the QMS and DSC service

A domain user called **QVService** has been established on the domain and has
been added to the local administrators group on Server1, and then logged in before
starting the installation. It is not critical, but I generally recommend logging in as
this user to perform the installation.

These are the steps to install the **QlikView Management Service (QMS)** and
Directory Services Connector (DSC) services on Server1:

1. Locate the installation file on the server, QlikViewServer_xYYSetup.exe
    (YY is 32 bit or 64 bit depending on the server), and double-click on the file
    to kick it off.

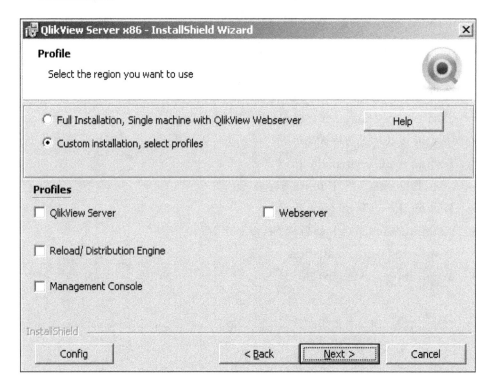

2. Click on **Next >** through all of the dialogs, as previously shown, until you
    arrive at the **Profiles** screen. Select the **Custom installation, select profiles**
    option. The different profile options become available on the screen.

    We will not be using these profiles right now (clicking on the **Help** button
    will tell you what each profile does), because they do not exactly match our
    requirement to install the QMS and the DSC on this server.

Click on the **Config** button (in the lower-left side of the wizard) to set the custom option.

3. Turn off all of the options except for **QlikView Directory Service Connector** and **QlikView Management Service**, as shown in the preceding screenshot. Click on the **Next** button.

4. Continue and enter the credentials for the QlikView service user.

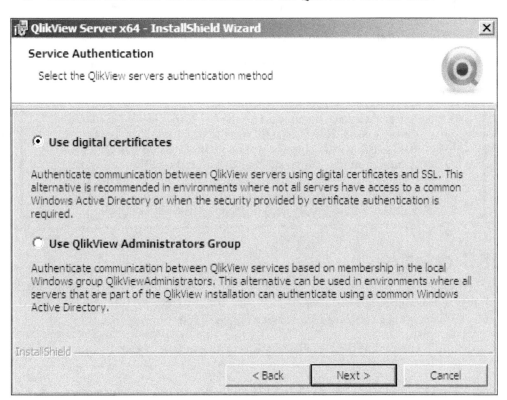

5. As shown in the preceding screen, select the **Use digital certificates** option (note that this screen does not appear on Window Server 2003). Click on **Next >**, and then click on the **Install** button that appears on the next screen. Once the installation is complete, restart the server.

 If you want to perform an installation without certificates, just leave the default option of **Use QlikView Administrators Group** and continue with the rest of the installation.

Testing the services installation

By selecting the **Use digital certificates** option in the installation process, some configuration changes will have been made. We can check them now.

QMC config

Locate the `QVManagementService.exe.config` file, which is colocated with the `QVManagementService.exe` file. By default, this will be installed at `C:\Program Files\QlikView\Management Service`, but that depends on the installation location chosen earlier.

Open this file in Notepad or any other text editor, look for the `UseWinAuthentication` entry, and double-check that it is set to `false`.

 Ignore this check if you went for the **Use QlikView Adminstrators Group** option. However, if this is not `false` (perhaps, because it is an existing installation or you accidentally chose **Use QlikView Adminstrators Group** instead of **Use digital certificates** during the installation), then you can manually set the value in the file, but you will need to stop the service first. Alternatively, you can do a quick uninstall and re-install, and choose the correct option.

DSC config

Locate the `QVDirectoryServiceConnector.exe.config` file, which is colocated with the `QVDirectoryServiceConnector.exe` file. By default, this will be located at `C:\Program Files\QlikView\Directory Service Connector`.

Again, double-check that the `UseWinAuthentication` entry is set to `false`.

Server certificates

Run **Microsoft Management Console** (MMC.exe) , and add (*Ctrl* + *M*) the **Certificates/Computer Account** for the local computer.

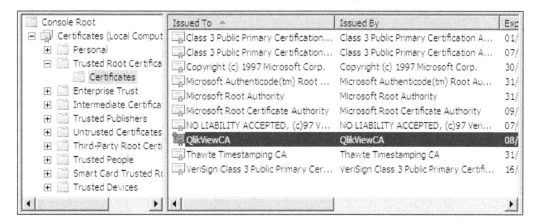

Confirm that the **QlikViewCA** certificate is listed under the Trusted Root Certificates folder, as shown in the preceding screenshot. Under **Personal**, you should see a certificate for the local server and for **QVProxy**.

Establishing the shared folder

For QlikView clustering, the server root and document folders must be on a shared folder, so that all members of the cluster will have access to the same documents. This share must be from a Windows Server — folders shared directly from SAN or NAS devices are not supported. If you are using a SAN device, it must be mounted to a Windows Server and the folders must be shared from this Server.

For our purpose, using Server1 to host this share will be ideal. It is critical, however, that there be extremely low latency between this share and the QlikView Servers, which are writing to and reading from the files. Effectively, this means that the cluster servers and the share server must be colocated on the same fast network.

 If you want to have servers in different countries to improve the speed for users in those countries, then clustering will not be the correct solution. Instead, you will have to deploy standalone servers in the different countries, and use QlikView Publisher (or just a batch file) to distribute documents to the different servers.

Follow these steps to create the folder structure:

1. Create a new folder on the server named QVS. The owner of this folder should be the QVService user (default if you are logged in as this user when creating the folder), and the QVService user should have full read-and-write access to the folder.

2. Share this folder, as QVS, with full read-and-write access for the QVService user.

3. Create a subfolder in this folder named Root.

4. As discussed earlier, create subfolders under QVS for each of the business areas that will have documents published. I will also create a UserApp folder under each of these subfolders. This is not entirely necessary, but it replicates the structure that I use in my development environment.

Installing the QVS service

As mentioned earlier, it is generally recommended to log in as the QVService user to perform the installation. Again, we need to take custom options for the installation, as the default profile for QlikView Server also includes the Directory Service Connector.

Let us now install the QVS services on Server2 and Server3, as shown in the following steps:

1. As before, locate the installation file on the server, and double-click on the file to kick it off.

2. Follow the prompts until you get to the **Profiles** screen. As before, select the **Custom installation, select profiles** option, and then click on the **Config** button. Deselect everything except **QlikView Server** and, optionally, **QlikView Server Example documents** (although, the only purpose here would be to extract them from the installer as reference documents). Click on **Next**.

3. Enter the QVService user credentials and click on **Next**. As before, on the **Service Authentication** screen, select the **Use digital certificates** option, and then click on **Next**.

4. On the final screen, click on **Install**. When the installation is complete, restart the server.

5. Repeat steps one to four on Server3.

Testing the QVS installation

As before, the base configuration to support the certificate authentication should have been established during the installation; so, this is just a quick test to ensure that all is OK.

The Settings file

Locate the `Settings.ini` file in the `ProgramData\QlikTech\Server` folder.

Check the **EnableSSL** setting is set to 1 (`EnableSSL = 1`). If this is not set to 1, it means that either something has gone wrong in the installation, or you have missed a step above. You should perform a quick uninstall and retry the installation with the correct options.

Installing the QDS (Publisher) service

As earlier, log in as the QVService user for this installation.

These are the steps to install the QDS service on Server4:

1. As before, locate the installation file on the server, and double-click on the file to kick it off. Follow the prompts until you get to the **Profiles** screen.

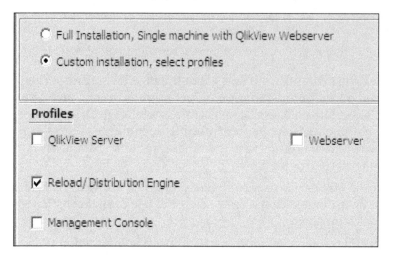

2. This time, we can just click on the **Reload/Distribution Engine** option under **Profiles**. Click on **Next**.
3. Enter the credentials as before, click on **Next**, and then select **Use digital certificates**. Click on **Next**, and then click on **Install**.
4. Once the installation is complete, restart the server.

Testing the QDS installation

Again, the base configuration to support the certificate authentication should have been established during the installation; so, this is just a quick test to ensure that all is OK.

QDS config

Locate the QVDistributionService.exe.config file, which is colocated with the QVDistributionService.exe file. By default, this will be located at C:\Program Files\QlikView\Distribution Service.

Again, double-check that the UseWinAuthentication entry is set to false.

Creating the Publisher folders

The Publisher server will perform all of the reloads and then distribute the final QVW files to QlikView Server. So, while we only need the UserApp folders on the QVS, we will need all of the folder sets (as discussed in the *QVS folder structure* section in *Chapter 3, Exploring the QlikView Management Console in Detail*) on the Publisher.

Follow these steps to establish the Publisher folders:

1. Connect to the QDS server (Server4).

2. Create a new folder on the server named QVP. As with the server folders on Server1, the owner of this folder should be the QVService user (default if you are logged in as this user when creating the folder), and the QVService user should have full read-and-write access to the folder.

3. Create a subfolder in this folder named Sales. Within Sales, create subfolders named UserApp, Loader, QVD, and Sources.

4. Create a new folder under QVP named Finance, and create the same set of subfolders as per the Sales folder. Repeat the same for HR. Essentially, you are creating the same folder structure that is in your development environment.

Installing the QlikView Web Service on IIS

Because our Web Service is standalone, and not a part of the domain, we cannot use the same QVService domain user that we used on all of the other servers. Instead, I have created a local user on that server called `QVService.local`, which will run the services. This user is added to the local administrators group on Server5.

These are the steps to install the Web Service on IIS on Server5:

1. As before, locate the installation file on the server, and double-click on the file to kick it off. Follow the prompts until you get to the **Profiles** screen, as follows:

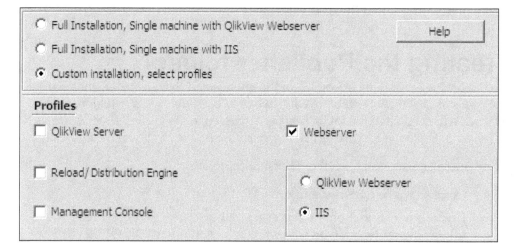

2. Note that the installer has added options for IIS, as it has detected that IIS is installed on the server. Select the **Webserver** option under **Profiles**, and then select the **IIS** option. Click on **Next** .

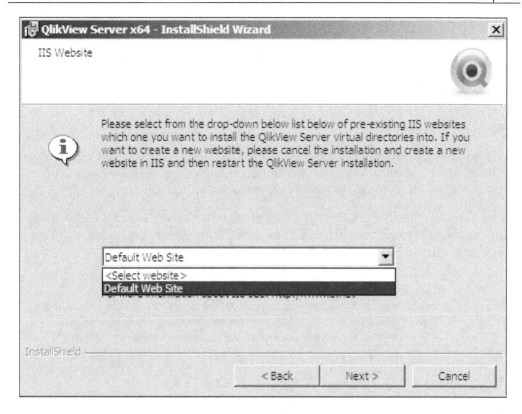

3. On the website screen, select the website that you are going to install. If there is only one website, select the **Default Web Site** option. Click on **Next**.

4. Enter the credentials for the local QVService user, and click on **Next**. Select **Use digital certificates**. Click on **Next**, and then click on **Install**.

5. Once the installation is complete, restart the server.

Testing the web installation

There are a few items that we need to check, to confirm that the Web Services are all configured correctly.

QSS config

When QlikView is installed on IIS, a new service called **QlikView Settings Service (QSS)** is installed to manage the settings via QMS. This service works off the same ports as QVWS.

Locate the `QVWebServerSettingsService.exe.config` file, which is colocated with the `QVWebServerSettingsService.exe` file. By default, this will be located at `C:\Program Files\QlikView\Server\Web Server Settings`.

As before, double-check that the `UseWinAuthentication` entry is set to `false`.

IIS settings

In IIS, an **application pool** is a collection of resources and settings that can be shared by different web applications. The installation should have added one application pool, QlikView IIS. It should also have created four virtual folders.

Check in the application pools for the website to ensure there is a new application pool called `QlikView IIS`. This should be a v4.0 Framework, integrated, pool, and the identity should be the local QVService user.

If you find that the application pool has not picked up the v4.0 Framework, and you are sure that the v4.0 Framework has been installed; it may be that IIS was installed after the v4.0 Framework. You should be able to register the correct version of the framework to IIS by running:

```
%windir%\Microsoft.NET\Framework64\v4.0.30319\aspnet_
regiis.exe -i
```

The following folders should have been added:

Folder	Path	Application pool
QlikView	C:\Program Files\QlikView\Web\	DefaultAppPool
QvAjaxZfc	C:\Program Files\QlikView\Server\ QlikViewClients\QlikViewAjax\	QlikView IIS
QvPlugin	C:\Program Files\QlikView\Server\ QlikViewClients\QlikViewPlugin\	DefaultAppPool
Scripts	C:\Program Files\QlikView\Server\ QvTunnel\	DefaultAppPool

Depending on your configuration, you may need to look at the application pool for other folders, but for `QvAjaxZfc`, it should be `QlikView IIS`. The other folders will have anonymous access—all of the security is handled via the `authenticate.aspx` page in the `QvAjaxZfc` folder.

Website

Open Internet Explorer and connect to `http://localhost/qlikview`. The website should open, but you should get a **No Server** message—this is fine, because we haven't connected all of the servers yet.

> Google Chrome will work out of the box for this also. Other browsers may prompt for a Windows username and password, although they can be configured to forward NTLM (**Single Sign-on**).

Connecting servers to QMS

When you install all of the services on one box, they are all automatically connected to QMS. In this case, we have installed services on several servers; so, we must tell the QMS where each of the services are located. We will also need to establish secure connections using certificates.

Directory Service Connector

We installed the DSC on the same server as the QMS, so that the service will already have the same server certificates as that of QMS.

A quick way to confirm that this is running using certificates is to use Internet Explorer to connect to the service address, and confirm that you get a **WSDL (Web Services Description Language)** response. The service address on Server1 is `https://server1:4730/DSC/Service`.

Without certificates, the service address for the DSC will be `http://server1:4730/DSC/Service`. This address should fail to connect when certificates are in use.

QlikView Servers

Now, we need to attach two servers. We will attach and configure the first for the shared settings, and then we simply add the second server.

A mistake many people make when they have a cluster license is to add the first server in the QMC, and then add the second server in the same way. This is incorrect. We should add the first server, and then add the second server within the properties of the first server (this addition does not imply any precedence).

To attach the QlikView servers to QMS, perform the following steps:

1. Connect to Server1 and open the QMS (`http://localhost:4780/qmc/Default.htm`). This is the first time we are connecting to Server1, and we will be told that the two services are down. This is correct because the QMS thinks that QVS and QVWS are on Server1.

2. Click on the **System** tab. Under **Setup**, click on **QlikView Servers**.

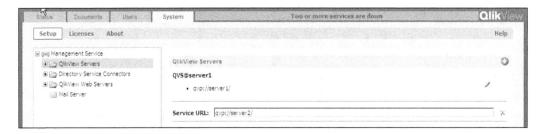

3. Click on the **+** button to add a new server. Enter the server address: `qvp://server2/`. Click on **Apply**.

4. For the moment, ignore the details presented in the dialog box for the certificates installation . At this stage, you can click on the **X** to the right of the `qvp://server1` entry (which is invalid) to remove it, and click on **Apply**. You will get a second dialog box with a new password (you get one password every time you click on **Apply**). Note this information in the following screenshot:

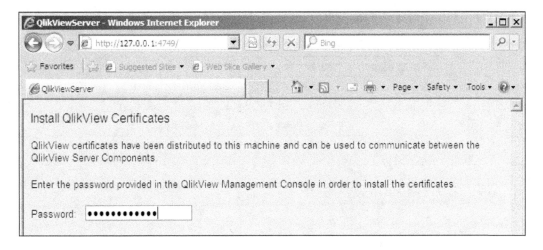

5. Connect to the first QlikView Server (Server2), open Internet Explorer, and enter the address specified in the message. Enter the password and press *Enter*. You should see a message stating that the certificates were successfully installed and unlocked.

    You can use the MMC.exe file, using the same procedure specified earlier, to view that the computer certificates have been installed.

6. Return to the QMS server and QMC. Click on the **System** tab. Under **Licenses**, add the server license (exactly as we did in *Chapter 2, Standard Installation Process*).

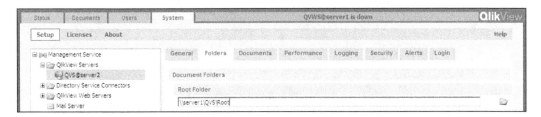

7. Navigate back to the **Setup** screen, expand QlikView Servers, and select **QVS@server2**. Click on the **Folders** tab and set the **Root Folder** field to the share that we created earlier — \\server1\QVS\Root. Click on **Apply**. Click on **OK** on the dialog box to restart the QVS.

8. Add the following mounts to the application folders, which we created in the share:

Mount name	Path
Sales	\\server1\QVS\Sales\UserApp
Finance	\\server1\QVS\Finance\UserApp
HR	\\server1\QVS\HR\UserApp

Click on **Apply**.

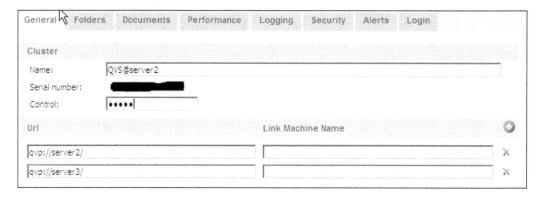

9. Click on the **General** tab. Click on the **+** button, and add the URI for the second QlikView Server: `qvp://server3/`. Insert the license **Control** number and click on **Apply**. Click on **OK** on the dialog box to restart the QlikView Server. Record the URL and password information that is needed to install the certificates on Server3.

   Note that the SetLicence procedure may not work correctly at this stage. However, continue with step 10.

10. Connect to the second QlikView Server (Server3) and open Internet Explorer. Enter the URL and password from the message shown earlier. The certificates should be installed as done earlier.

    If the SetLicence procedure failed in step 9, repeat it now on the QMS server and it should work correctly.

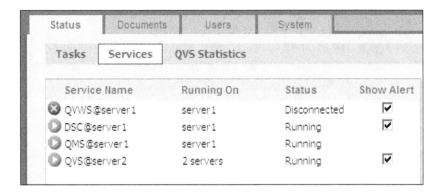

The QlikView Servers are now connected correctly and clustered. Under the **Status** tab, you should see only one QVS listed with a **Running On** value of **2 servers**.

QlikView Distribution Server – Publisher

Before we can add a QDS, we need to add the license in the QMC. Without a license, there isn't a separate management process for the reload engine outside of QVS; so, we can't add or modify the settings.

Once we add the license, we can easily add the new server (Server4) and remove the old one (Server2), if we have a clustered Publisher license. If we only have a single Publisher license, we will need to tweak some configuration files.

Follow these steps to add the QDS to the QMS:

1. In the Management Console, click on the **System** tab and then click on **Licenses**. Click on QlikView Publisher. This will show as **QDS@server1**, but we don't need to worry about that now. Enter the serial number, control number, name, and company as usual. If the server is not connected to the Internet, enter the **LEF** (**License Enabler File**) that has been provided by your QlikView Partner or directly from QlikTech. Click on **Apply License**.

2. Before we configure the next step, please note that you should, in general, never manually edit the **QVPR** (**QlikView Publisher Repository**). However, it is necessary in this special circumstance, where we only have the single Publisher license, and QMS does not present either a **+** button for us to add additional distribution services, nor does it allow us to delete the default option.

Stop the QlikView Management Service service on Server1.
Locate the QVPR folder; the default location is `C:\ProgramData\`
`QlikTech\ManagementService\QVPR`. Make a backup copy of the
`DistributionService.xml` file. Edit the original `DistributionService.`
`xml` file, and remove the whole `DistributionService` key.

Restart QlikView Management Service.

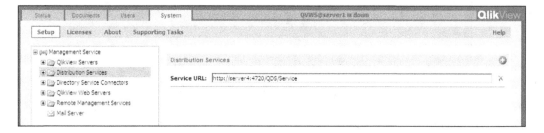

3. Click on **Setup**, then click on the `Distribution Services` folder. Click on
the **+** button in the **General** tab. Enter the **Service URL** value for the QDS:
`http://server4:4720/QDS/Service`.

   Click on **Apply**. Record the URL and password needed to install the
   certificates on Server4.

4. Connect to Server4. Run Internet Explorer, open the certificate URL,
and enter the password. You should get the message, **The password
was correct, QDS service at port 4720 is now unlocked**.

5. Connect to the Management Console, open the `Distribution Services`
folder, and click on **QDS@server4**.

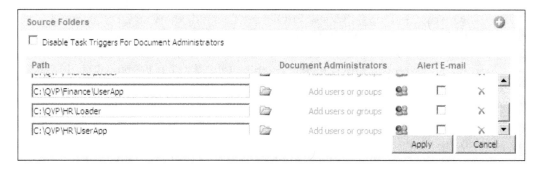

Click on the **+** button beside **Source Folders**, add the folders for your implementation, and then click on **Apply**. For this demonstration, the following folders are used:

Folder
C:\QVP\Sales\Loader
C:\QVP\Sales\UserApp
C:\QVP\Finance\Loader
C:\QVP\Finance\Loader
C:\QVP\HR\Loader
C:\QVP\HR\UserApp

QlikView Web Server

Because the web server is not on the same domain and may be in a different firewall zone, it is important to ensure that some ports are open between the QMS server and the web server. They are as follows:

Port	Description
4780	QlikView Management Service
4730	Directory Service Connector
4750	QlikView Webserver / Settings Service

In addition, the QVS port needs to be opened between the web server and QlikView Server.

Port	Description
4747	QlikView Protocol QVP

The previously mentioned ports need to be opened in both directions.

Follow these steps to connect the web server to the QMS:

1. Click on the **System** tab. Under **Setup**, click on the `QlikView Web Servers` folder:

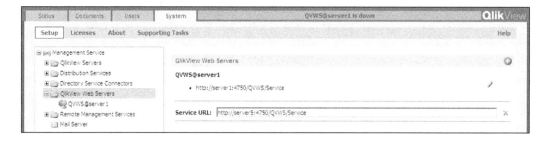

2. Click on the **Add** (+) button and enter the **Service URL** value for setting the service on Server5: `http://server5:4750/QVWS/Service`

    Click on **Apply**.

3. Ignore the certificate information for now. Click on the **X** symbol beside the Server1 entry to remove it. Click on **Apply**. This time, record the certificate installation URL and password.

4. Connect to the web server and run Internet Explorer. Open the certification URL and enter the password. You should get the message, **The password was correct, QVWS service at port 4750 is now unlocked**.

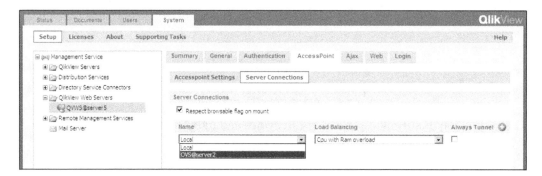

5. Open out the `QlikView Web Servers` folder and click on **QVWS@server5**. Click on the **AccessPoint** tab and the **Server Connections** button. Click on the **Name** dropdown, and change **Local** to **QVS@server2**. Leave the **Load Balancing** value as **Cpu with Ram overload**. Click on **Apply**.

Note, the web server will now open AccessPoint, but it will not present any documents. This is because we haven't changed the default security from NTFS, and the web server is in a different domain to the QlikView Server. We will look at alternative authentication options in *Chapter 7, Alternative Authentication and Authorization Methods*.

Summary

There has been quite a bit of information in this chapter. We have installed different services on multiple servers, and made sure they can communicate without having to be part of the same domain.

It is important to understand that while this is a good option for implementing QlikView across multiple servers, it is possible to implement on fewer servers (as we have seen in *Chapter 2, Standard Installation Process*, we can implement all of them on only one server) by selecting different custom options during installation, and configuring the correct options within the QMC. In this demonstration, we looked at installing only one web server, but we can have as many as we need. Often, companies will install two or three web servers, and use a **Network Load Balancer** (**NLB**) device to control which web server a user connects to.

In the next chapter, we will look in detail at the Publisher settings and how to configure different reload options.

6
Configuring the QlikView Publisher

Without a QlikView Publisher license, the **Reload Engine** must sit on the same server as the QlikView Server, and it can only perform a reload of a QlikView document in the server folders with a restricted set of triggers. When we have a QlikView Publisher license, the **Reload Engine** transforms to being the **QlikView Distribution Service (QDS)**, and we are no longer tied to the QlikView Server for reloads. The QDS can now be installed on its own server and many more task options become available. In this chapter, we will look at the configuration options for QDS, and look at the methods to create a couple of the more common tasks—reload as well as loop and reduce with manual distribution and automatic distribution, respectively.

The following topics are covered in this chapter:

- Exploring QMC Publisher components in detail. This includes the following topics:
    - ° System setup
    - ° Section Access Management
    - ° Source Documents
    - ° Supporting Tasks

- Creating tasks. These tasks include:
    - ° Reloading with manual distribution
    - ° Looping and reducing with automatic distribution

Exploring QMC Publisher components in detail

We have installed QDS a couple of times now—once as part of a single QlikView Server installation and once as part of an enterprise installation on its own server (Server4). When we add the Publisher license, the QDS changes from a simple reload engine to the fully-functional QlikView Publisher. This process adds a number of tabs into the QMC. We have already seen some of these during the initial setup and configuration in the previous chapter. Now, we will look at the new tabs in detail.

System setup

In the previous chapter, we saw some of the system setups, where we configured the folders for the Publisher on the **General** tab. We will have a look at this tab a bit more now, as well as the other tabs.

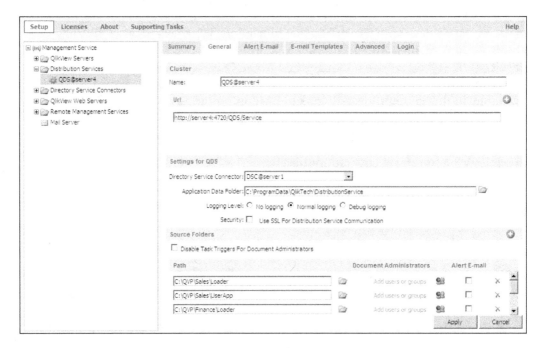

General

On the **General** tab, we have already seen the **Source Folders** option, where we added several folders that we had configured to hold our QVW files (refer to the *Creating the Publisher folders* section in *Chapter 5, Installing QlikView Server Enterprise*). Any folder added here (and its subfolders) will appear in the **Source Documents** tab, where we can configure various jobs.

There are several options that we can configure for each folder. We can add a list of document administrators who can log in to QMC, but they will only see information about the tasks and options around these folders, and not the system information. Selecting the **Alert E-mail** option will send alerts to these administrators. The **Disable Task Triggers For Document Administrators** option essentially means that the document administrators will neither be able to create or edit a trigger, nor cause a task to start.

Similar to QlikView Server, it is possible to have a cluster license for QlikView Publisher. Like QVS, to configure the cluster, we don't add additional **Distribution Services** entries; instead, we add the URLs for the additional services here under the **Cluster** option.

The other settings should be quite obvious. The **Application Data Folder** value is the setting that many administrators might want to change because it defaults to the c: drive, and administrators might prefer to have that on a different drive. This folder contains setting and logs.

Usually, it is not necessary to change the **Logging level** option from **Normal logging**. The **Debug logging** level can be useful for troubleshooting, but obviously adds additional load to the server.

The **Security** option is redundant in the enterprise configuration installed in the previous chapter, as the certificate-communication option happens by default.

Alert E-mail

The **Alert E-mail** option allows you to configure a number of e-mail addresses to receive alerts — basically when a task has failed.

You will need to make sure that you configure the **Mail Server** SMTP (in QMC, **System | Setup | Mail Server**) options, so that the e-mails can be sent. Here, you define whether e-mails are sent as HTML or in plain format.

E-mail Templates

There are a number of different templates that can be specified for the following conditions:

- **Alert**: This is used when a task has failed to alert the administrators
- **Notify**: This is used to notify recipients when a document has been distributed
- **Attachment**: This is used to send a QVW file to distribution recipients

There are two templates for each condition — one for HTML and one for plain text — depending on your **Mail Server** e-mail format's configuration.

Advanced

The **Advanced** tab has a couple of options on how many QlikView engines (QVB.exe) are used for different tasks. The QVB.exe file is essentially the same as the QV.exe file, except that it does not have a user interface. It can open documents and perform reloads and other tasks.

The options here for QVB are:

- **Distribution**: This option reloads and moves a document to different locations
- **Administration**: This option opens a document to retrieve settings and field values needed to configure tasks in QMC

Just as with any QlikView process, the more QVB processes you have open at the same time, the more memory and CPU resources are going to be used. If you have only a few QlikView administrators, then the **Administration** option isn't going to be a big problem. If you have many document administrators, who will be frequently changing options in the tasks, then it might be a problem. Similarly, if you have smaller documents and a low number of reload tasks, then the **Distribution** option won't be a consideration. If you have larger documents and frequent reloads, then it might become critical.

 Note, if you have set four reload engines and a fifth reload is scheduled to start, while four are already in process, then that fifth reload will wait for a period before timing out. You could solve this by increasing the number of reload engines to five, but that might cause a resource issue. It can be a fine balancing act. Often the best option is to just reschedule one or more of the tasks.

The **Send Workorder** option is something that you should rarely need to use. The workorder is an XML file that contains all of the task's information. It will be normally synchronized between the QMC and the QDS. If there is ever a problem with this synchronization, then you can choose to resend the work order here.

Section Access Management

When we add a Publisher license, a new option named **Section Access Management** becomes available under the **Users** tab.

This is a web service that delivers a table of data, which is managed via QMC. The design purpose of this table of data is to manage Section Access data (instead of using another source such as Excel or Access), but it can actually be used to hold any kind of data (for example, mapping tables).

The advantage of managing the information here, especially for Section Access information, is that it is security controlled. Access to the data is via a simple URL such as: `http://server1:4780/QMS/AuthTable`

However, this URL is secured using NTLM security to the members of the QlikView Administrators group. You should, therefore, note that this is not totally supported in a certificate-enabled system, and should only be used in a QlikView Administrators group system.

You can add as many tables as you need to have. This is useful when there are different Section Access configurations for different documents.

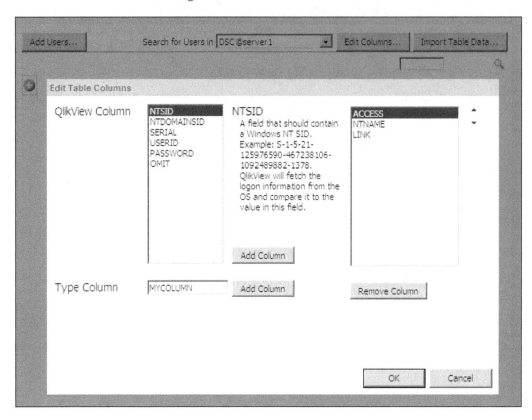

Within each table, you can define as many fields as you like. The standard Section Access fields are listed by default, but you can manually enter a name for a column and click on the **Add Column** button to add it, as shown in the preceding screenshot. You don't have to use the Section Access fields at all—your table can consist of only custom fields.

When adding values, the Section Access fields may have options such as a drop-down menu for the ACCESS column and a user selector for the NTNAME column, but most of the fields are just free text.

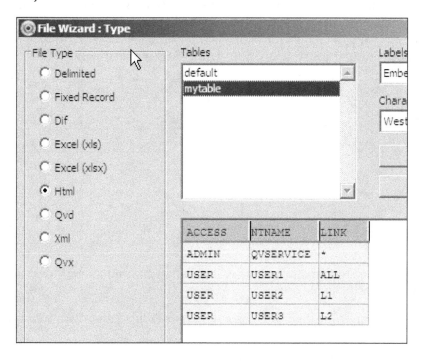

Accessing the tables is simply done by connecting to the URL within the script editor's table wizard and selecting the table to use. You can also choose **Insert | Section Access | Publisher Authorization** from the menus in the script editor – this ends up in the same place, but does allow you to save the URL in your user preferences.

Source Documents

Without a Publisher license, under the **Documents** tab, there is only a **User Documents** option. We previously used this tab to configure reload options, but if we look there now, there is no longer a **Reload** option. This is because reloads will no longer happen on the QlikView Server — they will happen on the Publisher server, and the properties are managed via the **Source Documents** tab.

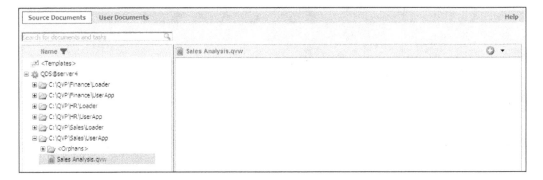

Under the **Source Documents** tab, we will see all of the folders that we previously configured under the QDS.

In the next section, we will use this tab to configure reload and distribute tasks.

Supporting Tasks

When we add the Publisher license, a new option named **Supporting Tasks** becomes available under the **System** tab.

Supporting tasks are jobs that are not linked to the documents, but may be necessary to support reload and distribution of QlikView documents.

The possible tasks are as follows:

Task type	Description
External program	This task will simply execute an external program or batch file. The main parameter is a path to the file to be executed. This can be used for many purposes. I have seen people using this to run a batch file that runs the QV.exe command line to reload tasks. This can be done to perform OnPostReload actions in a QVW file, as these are not executed by QDS reload tasks.

Task type	Description
Database command	This allows you to execute an SQL command against a specified connection string. There could be many reasons such as data cleansing, view creation, temporary table creation, and others. But obviously you need to be careful!
Pause	This does exactly what it says on the tin—pauses for either a specific length of time or until a specified time. These tasks can be chained with other reload or distribution tasks.
QVD creation	This allows us to specify a piece of script that will generate a table and then save that table to QVD. Any valid QlikView script will be acceptable. You can also specify a list of users to add security to the files. This can save you from creating QVWs just to generate QVDs.

Creating tasks

The main use of QlikView Publisher is to reload the documents, and then distribute them somewhere, all on a scheduled basis.

As described earlier, the reload task will use the **QlikView Batch (QVB)** executable file (QVB.exe) to execute the script and refresh the data in the file.

We also have the option to run a loop and reduce task across a field in the document, and create multiple versions of the document that only have the data associated with each field value. For example, we might select the **Sales Region** field, and the loop and reduce process will create one QlikView file for each region, each file only containing the data for that region.

Distribution is the process of moving the document to its final location. This could be a folder, an e-mail recipient, or mostly to a QlikView Server.

We will now look at creating reload and distribution tasks. We will examine a couple of different tasks as well as the commonly-used options.

Reloading a task with manual distribution

First, we will perform a reload, specify manual options for where the file will be placed, and what security will be placed on the file.

Follow these steps to perform a reload with manual distribution:

1. In QMC, click on the **Documents** tab and the **Source Documents** option.

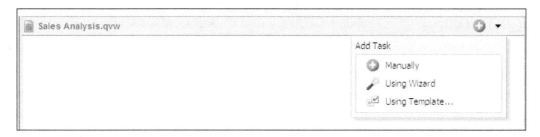

2. Open the folder that contains the document that you wish to reload, and select the document. Click the ▼ button on the far right of the screen and select **Using Wizard** from the drop-down menu.

3. In step 1 of the wizard, we are going to do everything manually and we will not do a reduction; so just click on **Next**.

4. In step 2, leave the name blank (a name will be generated) and click on **Next**.

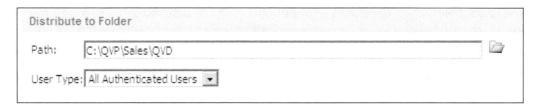

5. In step 3, enter a **Path** to which you want to distribute the file, and set the **User Type** value to **All Authenticated Users**, as shown in the preceding screenshot. Click on **Next**.

6. In Step 4, click on the **+** button and specify a daily reload at 08:00:00. Note, you can add as many triggers as you want. Click on **Finish** to complete the wizard.

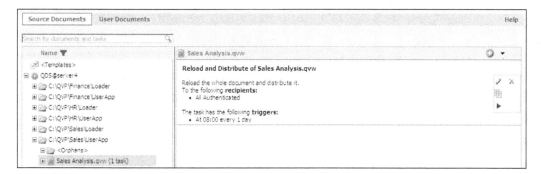

7. To test the task, click on the ► button.

And it is as simple as that!

Note, if you were to open the document that was distributed, then the script will be cleared and a comment will be displayed to say that this is because reload is disabled upon distribution. You can change this behavior in the document within QlikView Desktop by navigating to **Document Preferences | Security | Reload**.

This option is set on a QVW by QVW basis. For that reason, it is important to understand from where you are reloading a document and where you are distributing it to—you wouldn't want to overwrite your source document with a document that has an empty script!

Loop and reduce with automatic distribution

Next, we will look at creating a task manually and adding in many more options including loop and reduce, and using a field in the document to specify the authentication.

Follow these steps to add a loop and reduce task:

1. Select the same document as in the previous set of instructions (in the previous section). Instead of selecting the **Wizard** option to add a task, select **Manually**.

2. On the **General** tab, give a name to the task, such as `Reload of Sales Document`.

3. On the **Reload** tab, leave the reload option selected (it is interesting to note that you can also deselect it as a reload is not always required—the reload may have been done on a different task). We don't need to specify Section Access credentials (QlikView authentication) or specify a partial reload.

4. On the **Reduce** tab, click on the **Open Document** button. This causes the document to be opened in a `QVB.exe` session on the QDS server. Click on the pencil icon to the right of the **Reduced Document Name** option.

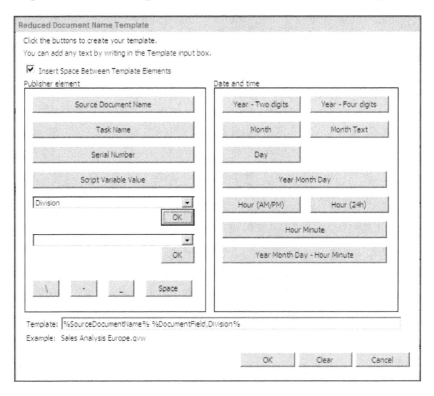

5. In the **Select Document** field's dropdown, select an appropriate field to reduce by, for example, **Division**. Click on the **OK** button under the field, and note that `%DocumentField,Division%` has been added to the **Template** field. Click on **OK** to close the dialog.

6. Ignore the **Simple Reduction** options. These allow you to select specific values to reduce on, but we will rarely need to select this option. Normally, we want to select all of the values in a field. Under the **Loop and Reduce** option, select the same field as in the previous step (**Division**). This will cause all of the values in this field to be used. This will be dynamic, as the values are added or removed after the task is created.

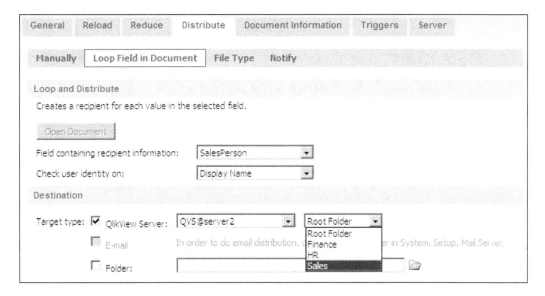

7. On the **Distribute** tab, select **Loop Field in Document**. Select a field, for example **SalesPerson**, in the application and a field in the directory on which that user can be looked up, for example, **Display Name**. Under **Destination**, select for **QlikView Server**, and select the correct QVS and folder from the drop-down menus.

8. On the **Document Information** tab, type `Sales` in the **Or Type a New Category** box.

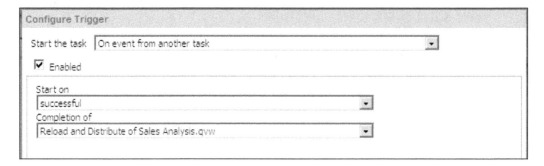

9. On the **Triggers** tab, add a new trigger. Select **On event from another task** from the drop-down menu, select **successful**, and then select the task from the previous step. Click on **OK** to close the dialog.

10. Click on **Apply** to save the task.

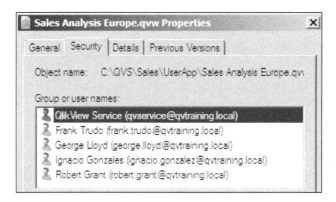

11. Execute the task. Several files should be created in the `server` folder. Checking the security on the files should reveal that only the QVService user and the appropriate users from the field value will have access to the file.

Summary

In this chapter, we have taken a good look at the options that can be configured for QlikView Publisher. We have configured some reload and distribution tasks, including a loop and reduce task.

In the next chapter, we will look at alternatives to **Active Directory** (**AD**) for authentication.

7
Alternative Authentication and Authorization Methods

What is the difference between authentication and authorization? When you log into your PC, your user credentials are checked against a user database (the local user database, Active Directory, LDAP, or other system), and you are let through to your desktop—this is authentication. When you try and open a file, the file system checks to see if you have the rights to open that file—this is authorization. You can see that authorization requires authentication to happen first, because authentication identifies the user who needs to be authorized.

We have already seen how we log into QlikView's AccessPoint with Active Directory/NTLM authentication, by allowing the credentials to be either automatically passed by the browser, or by entering the credentials in a standard challenge/response form. It is important to understand that the authentication step here is being performed by Windows, usually against Active Directory (Microsoft's implementation of a user repository). QlikView gets your identity from Windows, and then can authorize you to access QlikView Documents.

While Windows authentication will serve quite a lot of the world, many organizations do not deploy Active Directory, and instead use alternate directory services—such as ApacheDS **LDAP (Lightweight Directory Access Protocol)**—to store credentials for users. Even those companies that do deploy Active Directory, may need to give access to external people (sales people, directors, and so on), who may not have an Active Directory account. Even if the external user does have an Active Directory account, the IT department may not want to deploy an external website using Active Directory credentials.

Luckily, QlikView can be very flexible in the way it deals with authentication—basically, by not doing it. Except for Custom User authentication, QlikView does not handle the authentication process—it relies on a trusted external agency (such as Active Directory or a web portal) to perform the authentication, and then QlikView will deal with the authorization part—what QlikView documents does that user have access to.

As far as AccessPoint is concerned, the authentication process is brokered by a web application called `Authenticate.aspx`. Out of the box, this will handle the NTLM authentication automatically. It will also handle QlikView tickets (this will be discussed in more detail later in this chapter), HTTP header, and Custom User authentication. It does not handle any other type of authentication (for example, LDAP)—but you can write your own `Authenticate.aspx` to handle this.

It is outside the scope of this book to cover customizing the `Authenticate.aspx` file. There is a document called *Customized Authentication* available from QlikTech or your authorized partner that contains example code for this.

These are the topics we'll be covering in this chapter:

- Types of **Directory Service Provider (DSP)**
- Enabling DMS authentication and establishing ACLs in the QMC
    - ○ DMS Authorization options
- Configuring Directory Service Provider
    - ○ Configuring a Configurable ODBC DSP
    - ○ Configuring a Configurable LDAP DSP
    - ○ Configuring a Custom Directory DSP
- Enabling HTTP header authentication
- QlikView Ticket authentication

Types of Directory Service Provider (DSP)

Even if we are not authenticating against LDAP, we can have another party authenticate and use one of the other mechanisms to pass that authentication through to QlikView. For that reason, it is useful for us to be able to look up users and groups in the LDAP directory and retrieve a list of them.

QlikView can have several kinds of **Directory Service Providers (DSPs)**:

DSP type	Description
Active Directory	Connects to the Active Directory using LDAP calls—this is what we would have used by default in the **Manage Users** dialogs to retrieve users and groups. You can use either a fully-qualified domain name (FQDN) here—for example, LDAP://domain.local—or just the NetBIOS domain name—LDAP://DOMAIN. If you do use the FQDN, the DSC will resolve the NetBIOS name (in this case, DOMAIN) and use that as the DSP identifier. This means that any user identified as DOMAIN\USER will be linked with this DSP.
Custom Directory	A Custom Directory is a user and group repository that is maintained within the QlikView Management Console (actually, within the QVPR—the data repository that the QlikView Management services use to store settings). We will have a look at configuring this later.
Configurable ODBC	This is a repository of users and groups that is maintained in a separate database. There needs to be database tables or views established with particular fieldnames, but it is fairly straightforward. We will look at this later.
Configurable LDAP	This is a connection to an LDAP server used to resolve users and groups. We will show an implementation example later.
Local directory	This allows connection to the local server's user database to get users and groups.
Windows NT	Connects to a legacy Windows NT (pre 2000) domain.

Except for Custom Users, the authorization of users does not actually use any of these connections to authenticate a user. These connections serve to allow the administrators to add entries in the **ACLs (Access Control Lists)**, to assign licenses, and for the DSC to resolve a user's group memberships. We still need a separate, trusted process to do the authentication, and pass the user and group information.

There are actually two steps to the authorization process. First, the file access is checked against the ACL, and then Section Access is checked. The user will have to pass both tests before the file is listed in AccessPoint.

Before we do anything else, though, we are going to have to change QlikView's authentication mechanism from NTFS to DMS. This changes the way access to files is checked—from using the files' NTFS ACLs to using an Access Control List established in the QMC.

Enabling DMS authentication and establishing ACLs in the QMC

Before we can start authorizing users, other than by using the default of Active Directory users and NTFS **ACLs (Access Control Lists)**, we need to change the authorization method that QVS uses:

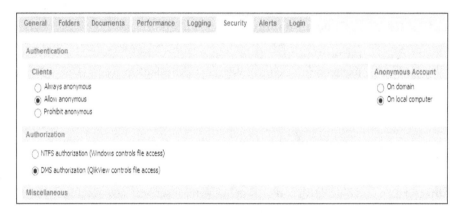

Follow these steps to enable DMS authorization:

1. Open the **QlikView Management Console** and navigate to **System | QlikView Servers | QVS@<servername>**, and click on the **Security** tab.

2. Change the **Authorization** setting from **NTFS authorization** to **DMS authorization**.

3. Click on **Apply**.

If you were to look at the AccessPoint at this stage, there would be no documents visible. We need to configure ACLs on a document-by-document basis.

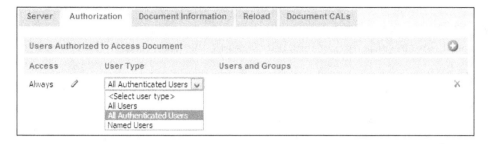

Follow these steps to establish the Access Control List for a document:

1. Navigate to the **Documents | User Documents** tab and select the document for which you want to set the ACL. Click on the **Authorization** tab (this tab was not available under NTFS mode).

2. Click on the **+** button to add a new **Access** row.

3. Under **User Type**, click on the drop-down list and select **All Authenticated Users** (see table in the next section for a description of the drop-down options).

4. Click on **Apply**.

The selected document should now be visible in AccessPoint.

DMS Authorization options

Let's look at the currently available options that we need to know about, as shown in the following screenshot:

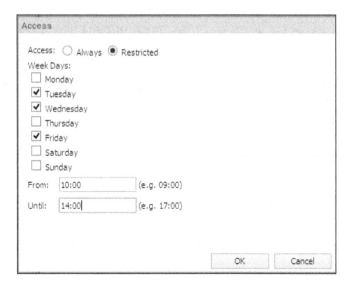

Under **Access**, we can click on the pencil button and specify either **Always** or **Restricted**. If you choose **Restricted**, then you get to specify the exact days of the week and time periods during which the users will have access to the document.

When we choose which users have access to the document, we have three options in the drop-down list:

Drop-down option	Description
All Users	This is effectively an **Anonymous** option. Anyone who can get to the server (via a portal for example) will pass the first authorization test (Section Access will still be in play).
All Authenticated User	For most implementations, this is pretty much the same as **All Users** as users must have been authenticated somehow.
Named Users	This allows you to specify the users or groups that will have access to the document, via the **Manage Users** dialog that we have used before.

Each row can have different user options and different users, or you could have multiple rows with the same users but with different sets of restrictions. Note that restrictions are additive — if one set of restrictions only gives you access on four days and a second set of restrictions gives you access on the other three days, then you will have access on all days.

Configuring Directory Service Providers

The Directory Service Providers are used for adding users and groups to document ACLs, assigning licenses to users, and resolving group memberships for users.

In this section, we will look at the options available to connect to a database user repository, an LDAP directory, and a QlikView Custom User repository. The Custom User repository is the only one for which QlikView manages the authentication process. The other two will require a third-party authentication, and either Custom Header or **Custom Ticket Exchange** (**CTE**), to pass the user information to QlikView.

All of the configurations explained in the following sections take place on the QMC **System** tab, under the `Directory Service Connectors` folder.

Configuring a Configurable ODBC DSP

The Configurable ODBC DSP allows you to point the DSC at a database. Any database engine with an ODBC driver (SQL Server, Access, Oracle, and so on) should work.

The database should have two tables (views will also work) that contain the entities—both users and groups—and the associations between them.

The `entity` table must have the following fields:

Field name	Description
entityid	A unique key field (integer) that is the primary key for this table. These keys will be used to associate users and groups.
name	The user or group ID—the ID that will be passed as part of the authentication message. For example, User1, jbloggs, Group1, and so on.
descr	The user or group description—a text description. For example, "John Doe", "Joe Bloggs", "Customer Group".
email	The e-mail address of the user. This is useful in conjunction with Publisher for the distribution of QVWs or PDFs.

The `groups` table has only two fields:

Field name	Description
groupid	An ID associated with `entityid` in the `entity` table that corresponds to a group.
memberid	An ID associated with `entityid` in the `entity` table that corresponds to a user.

Note, that there is no mechanism here to ensure that the `groupid` field points to a group and not a user, and vice versa with `memberid`. It is up to you to make sure that the associations are correct.

Configuring the DSP

Once the tables or views are established, we need to create the connection under the DSC's **Configurable ODBC** settings. Follow these steps to add the DSP:

1. Click on the **Configurable ODBC** option under **Directory Service Connectors**. Click on the **+** button. Enter the name of the server to which you are connecting, in the format:

   `ODBC://servername`

2. Enter the username and password to use.

3. Click on the **Apply** button, and then click on the pencil button to edit the settings. The available settings are as follows:

Setting	Description
Service timeout in seconds	The timeout before the DSC stops trying to connect to the DSP. The default is 30 seconds.
Directory label	This is the "domain name" for this DSP—it needs to be unique among DSPs. For example, I might use "CODBC" as this value. If the DSC has passed a user in the format "CODBC\username", it knows to use this DSP to try to resolve groups.
Entity name	This is the name of the field in the `entity` table that contains the user or group ID. As per the preceding table, this should be `name`.
Entity table db name	This is the name of the table or view that contains the entities. As per the preceding table, this should be `entity`.
Groups table db name	This is the name of the table or view that contains the entity-to-group associations. As per the preceding table, this should be `groups`.

Setting	Description
Data source name	This is the name of the ODBC driver that will be used to connect to the database. You can look in the ODBC manager to see the list of available names, or else have a look in the registry under HKLM\ SOFTWARE\ODBC\ODBCINST.INI, where you can see a list of the installed drivers. For example, if you are using SQL Server and the SQL Server 10 native client is installed, you should use **SQL Server Native Client 10.0.**
Conn db name	This is the name of the database on the server that contains the two tables or views. If I were setting up a specific database for this, I might call it something like QlikViewConfigurableODBC.
Database backend	I prefer to leave this as ODBC and use the connection details that I have established earlier. The other options are SQL and Oracle, which allows you to configure specific settings for those databases. However, the ODBC option will also work for SQL and Oracle databases, so I would just use that, and then I can change it more easily in the future.
Override connection string	This allows you to specify a separate connection string, which overrides all of the above settings. This can be useful for some databases. Otherwise, leave this blank.
Cache expiry in minutes	The DSC will query the user information when required, but will cache this information. This specifies for how long to cache the information.

4. Click on **Confirm** to close the dialog window, and then click on **Apply** again to save the changes.

5. If the connection is not successful, you will see an asterisk appear beside the connection. Hover over it to view the error message, which should give you guidance on how to resolve the issue.

Configuring a Configurable LDAP DSP

The **Configurable LDAP** option allows us to connect to an LDAP server to retrieve user information and resolve names. We need to establish some key facts with the LDAP administrators before we start. These facts are as follows:

Fact	Details
Name of the server and the dc that contains the users.	These will form the connection string to the server in the format: LDAP://ldapserver:port/ dc=example,dc=com.
Does the server support LDAP over SSL and what ports are used?	Common ports for unsecured connections are 389 and 10389. The default port for LDAP is 636.

Fact	Details
Credentials for the user that we are going to use when querying the LDAP.	The user will be expressed in the full LDAP distinguished name format—for example, `uid=admin,ou=system` or `uid=manager,dc=example,dc=com`.
The LDAP object classes for users and groups.	Common examples would be person, `inetOrgPerson`, `groupOfUniqueNames`, and so on.
The user ID property name.	Usually, this is `uid`.
The display name.	This might be `dn` or `displayName`.
The e-mail property.	Usually, this is `mail` or sometimes `e-mail`.
The group ID property name.	Quite often this is `cn`.
Distinguished name property.	This will be `dn` or `distinguishedName`.
How groups link to users?	Mostly, this will be implemented as `uniqueMember` values within the group containing the distinguished name of the user. However, sometimes it is implemented as a `memberOf` value in the user entry, pointing at the group name. This information is very important for QlikView to be able to resolve groups.

Configuring the DSP

To enter the **Configurable LDAP** DSP, follow these steps:

1. Click on the **Configurable LDAP** option under **Directory Service Connectors**. Click on the **+** button. Enter the name of the server to which you are connecting, in the format established earlier. Enter the username (full distinguished name) and password.

2. Click on **Apply** and then click on the pencil icon.

For a groupOfUniqueNames scenario using the **uniqueMember** option, here are the settings:

Setting	Description
Directory label	This is the "domain name" for this DSP—it needs to be unique among the DSPs. For example, I might use LDAP as this value. If the DSC has passed a user in the format "LDAP\username", it knows to use this DSP to try and resolve groups.
Service timeout in seconds	The timeout before the DSC stops trying to connect to the DSP. The default is 30 seconds.
Cache expiry in minutes	The DSC will query the user information when required, but will cache this information. This specifies how long to cache the information.
LDAP filter	This is optional, but it is useful to add in order to restrict the results returned by LDAP to just users and groups. The values in the filter depend on the facts that we gathered earlier, but something like this might work: (|(objectClass=inetOrgPerson)(objectclass= groupOfUniqueNames)).
Id property name	This is the unique ID for the user. Often, this will be uid.
Account name property name	Text name for the user. This will often be dn, or displayName, or something similar. It is used as part of the search when looking for users.
Display name property name	This is the value that will be returned by the search as the username. I have found that some LDAP's (for example, Apache DS) values are not handled correctly by QlikView when I use displayName (it just displays **byte[]** or similar), so I might just use uid in here.
E-mail property name	E-mail address field. This is used by Publisher for distribution.
User member of property name	We don't need this for this scenario, as we are not trying to resolve the memberOf property. Leave it blank.
User object class value	We should have established this earlier—value can be person or inetOrgPerson, among others.
Group / Member match property	This is the field value in the user entry that will be stored in the uniqueMember field in the group entry. Usually this will be dn or distinguishedName.
Group id property name	This is the unique ID for the group. Often, this will be cn.
Group member property name	This is the property in the group that stores the connection to the user. In the case of a groupOfUniqueNames, this is usually uniqueMember.
Group object class value	We should know this from the discussion earlier—the class of the group objects. Usually groupOfUniqueNames or groupOfNames.

The following is a screenshot of a sample entry:

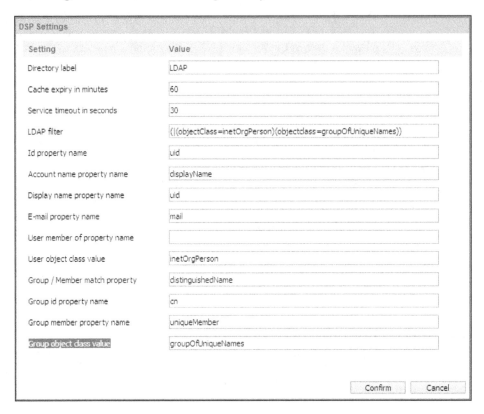

For a `memberOf` scenario, most of the values are the same. The ones that are different are shown in the following table:

Setting	Description
User member of property name	In this case, we need to specify the field in the user record that identifies the groups that a user is a member of. Usually, this is `memberOf`.
Group / Member match property	This is the field in the group entry whose value will be stored in the `memberOf` field in the user entry. Usually, this will be the group ID, so `cn`.
Group member property name	This should be blank, as we are not looking in the group to get the users.

1. Click on **Confirm** and then click on **Apply** to save.

2. If the connection is not successful, you will see an asterisk appear beside the connection. Hover over it to view the error message, which should give you guidance on how to resolve the issue.

Configuring a Custom Directory DSP

The Custom Directory DSP is an XML repository maintained by the DSC.
It is a simple database of users and groups. To add a new Custom Users DSP,
perform the following steps:

1. Click on the **Custom Directory** option under **Directory Service Connectors**.
   Click on the + button. Enter the name of the DSP — this is our "domain
   name" for this DSP, it needs to be unique among other DSPs. For example,
   I might use CUSTOM as this value. If the DSC has passed a user in the format
   "CUSTOM\username", then it knows to use this DSP to try and resolve
   groups. You don't need to enter a username and password at this time.

2. Click on **Apply**, and then click on the **Users** tab that has now appeared.

3. Click on the + button to start adding users. Enter appropriate information in
   the four textboxes, and remember to check the **Enabled** checkbox. Don't try
   to add any groups to the users at this stage, as we haven't established any
   groups yet.

4. Once you have added a number of users, click on the **Apply** button.

5. Click on the + button to add groups. Enter a group name, and then click on
   the **Manage Users** button to add users to this group. Note that, as explained
   earlier, you can use wildcards or just *, to search for users.

6. Click on **Apply** when you have finished adding groups.

Testing DSPs

We can't directly test the authentication, but we can test that the DSC can query the DSPs and resolve users and groups.

Follow these steps to test your DSPs:

1.   In the QMC, click on the **Users** tab.

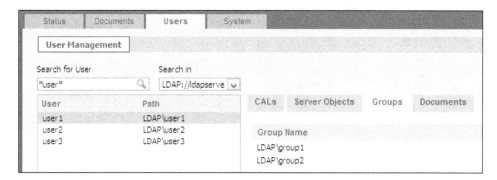

2.   Enter a search term and select one of your DSPs from the drop-down list. Check that the server returns a list of users and resolves groups.

    Note that you can simply use * as the search term to return all valid objects. You can also enter a list of users, separated by semicolons, to search for more than one user at a time.

Testing Custom Directory authentication

To test the Custom Directory authentication, we need to reconfigure the AccessPoint portal to expect custom users, and also to present a form for authentication.

The following steps show you how to test Custom Directory authentication:

1.   In QMC, click on the **System** tab, expand **QlikView Web Servers**, and then select your web server. Click on the **Authentication** tab.

2. Set the **Authentication** option to **Login**, and set **Type** to **Custom User**. The **Prefix** parameter of **Parameters** should match the DSP name established earlier—for example, CUSTOM\). Set **Login Address** to **Alternate login page (web form)**. Click on **Apply**.

3. Open a web browser and connect to your AccessPoint, for example, http://server5/qlikview. You should be redirected to the FormLogin.htm, as shown below page.

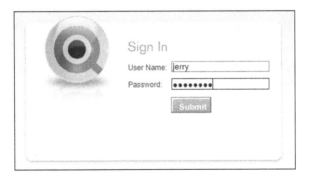

4. Enter a custom user's login credentials and you should be logged into AccessPoint as that user. It should even retrieve the user's full name and display it.

5. If you were to check the logfile for the Directory Service Connector (refer to *Chapter 8, Monitoring and Troubleshooting QlikView Server*, for more information on logfiles), you would see something like this:

```
Start web service call ResolveGroups for user CUSTOM\jerry
Resolved 2 groups for CUSTOM\jerry: CUSTOM\Group1 CUSTOM\Group2
```

You can see that the DSC has called the DSP to resolve the group memberships for the user.

Enabling HTTP header authentication

HTTP header authentication allows a third-party service, for example Apache Web Server, to perform an authentication — using whatever mechanism it chooses — and then pass the username through to QlikView by injecting an HTTP header into the packet being sent to AccessPoint.

To enable this, we need to reconfigure the AccessPoint authentication:

1. In QMC, click on the **System** tab, expand **QlikView Web Servers**, and then select your web server. Click on the **Authentication** tab.

2. Set the **Authentication** option to **Login**, set the **Type** to **Header**, and set **Login Address** to **Alternate login page (web form)**. The **Header Name** parameter, which defaults to **QVUSER**, is the name of the HTTP header that needs to be injected. The **Prefix** parameter should match one of the DSP names established earlier — for example, CUSTOM\ or LDAP\). Click on **Apply**.

3. The next step is dependent on your third-party product. For Apache, you would edit the `httpd.conf` file to include proxy and reverse proxy entries to the `/qlikview` and `/qvajaxzfc` virtual folders on the QlikView Web Server, perform an authentication against the `authenticate.aspx` location, and then pass the authenticated user in the header — something like this:

```
RequestHeader add QVUSER "%{AUTHENTICATE_uid}e"
```

 Typically, many of these frontends will implement reverse proxy — they receive a request with an address that ends in /qlikview or /qvajazafc, and they forward that to the QlikView Web Server. As far as the user is concerned, they are not talking to a different server.

QlikView ticket authentication

QlikView has had a **Custom Ticket Exchange** (**CTE**) mechanism since Version 9. Prior to Version 11, this mechanism was run by executing a COM call on the QlikView Server and retrieving a time-limited ticket. By attaching the ticket to the URL used to open a document, it identified the user to QlikView Server. There was a limitation in that the ticket could only authenticate a user to one document (using the `qvajaxzfc/opendoc.htm` page).

Since Version 11.0, a new mechanism has been introduced whereby, a ticket is obtained by making a web service call to the QlikView Server. This ticket can now be used to authenticate the user not to individual files but to AccessPoint.

The use case would be that a trusted server would authenticate the user (for example, via LDAP, Oracle SSO, and so on), make a request to the QlikView Web Server, obtain a ticket, and then redirect the user to the QlikView Web Server with the ticket encoded in the URL.

The trust mechanism is simply based on the IP address.

Enable CTE server authentication

To enable CTE server authentication, we need to do just a few things:

1. Open the `config.xml` file in `C:\ProgramData\QlikTech\WebServer`.
2. Locate the entry for `GetWebTicket` and change it from:

   ```
   <GetWebTicket url="/QvAjaxZfc/GetWebTicket.aspx" />
   ```

   to:

   ```
   <GetWebTicket url="/QvAjaxZfc/GetWebTicket.aspx">
   <TrustedIP>192.168.0.2</TrustedIP>
   <TrustedIP>192.168.0.3</TrustedIP>
   </GetWebTicket>
   ```

3. The IP addresses listed are the addresses of servers that are allowed to request a ticket. These can be either IPv4 or IPv6 addresses.
4. Save the file. Stop and restart the QlikView Web Server service for the changes to take effect.

Note, that if you are using IIS, you can implement alternate security on the `GetWebTicket.aspx` file, for example, by using certificates.

There is a document called *Customized Authentication* available from QlikTech or your authorized partner, that contains more detailed information about this process than we can go into here.

Requesting a ticket

Requesting a ticket is fairly straightforward. We need to send an HTTP POST request to the `GetWebTicket.aspx` page, with some XML, in this simple format:

```
<Global method="GetWebTicket">
<UserId>LDAP\USER1</UserId>
</Global>
```

Or, if you want to include groups:

```
<Global method="GetWebTicket">
<UserId>LDAP\USER1</UserId>
<GroupList>
<string>LDAP\Group1</string>
<string>LDAP\Group2</string>
</GroupList>
<GroupsIsNames>true</GroupsIsNames>
</Global>
```

Note, that both the user and group names are prefixed with the label for the DSP that they are associated with. Also note that if you pass a list of groups, the DSC will not try to resolve any other groups for this user.

The result should look something like the following lines of code:

```
<Global>
<_retval_>fbXiktaZQUv/bNvByJMDx6MTkbyBzp/6ggfBk84i</_retval_>
</Global>
```

The return value should be a 40-character sequence of characters—this is the ticket.

Downloading the example code

You can download the example code files for all Packt books you have purchased from your account at http://www.packtpub.com. If you purchased this book elsewhere, you can visit http://www.packtpub.com/support and register to have the files e-mailed directly to you.

Ticket testing of VBScript

The following code is VBScript code that can be used to test the implementation of ticketing. It will request a ticket, parse the response XML, and then open Internet Explorer with the generated URL:

```
Option Explicit

' Establish some variables
Dim sServer, sSuccessURL, sFailURL
Dim sUser, sGroups, sGroupList
Dim sURL, sRequest, sResult, sTicket
Dim iStart

' Name of our QlikView Web Server
sServer="localhost"
' URL to use if ticket is successful - AccessPoint
sSuccessURL = "http://localhost/qlikview"
' URL to use if the ticket fails
sFailURL="http://localhost/qlikview/FormLogin.htm"

' User to get ticket for
sUser = "LDAP\user1"
' Semicolon separated list of groups that user is a member of
sGroups = "LDAP\group1;LDAP\group2"

' Parse Out the Group List
sGroupList = ""

if sGroups <> "" Then
  Dim arr, sGroup
  arr = split(sGroups, ";")

  sGroupList = "<GroupList>"

  for each sGroup in arr
    sGroupList = sGroupList & "<string>" & sGroup & "</string>"
  Next

  sGroupList = sGroupList & "</GroupList>"
  sGroupList = sGroupList & "<GroupIsNames>true</GroupIsNames>"
End if
```

```
' URL for the GetWebTicket service
sUrl = "http://" & sServer & "/QvAJAXZfc/GetWebTicket.aspx"
' XML request
sRequest = "<Global method=""GetWebTicket""><UserId>" & _
  sUser & "</UserId>" & sGroupList & "</Global>"

sResult = HTTPPost (sUrl, sRequest)
sTicket = ""

' Look for the XML _retval_ tag
iStart = Instr(sResult, "<_retval_>")

' If it's there, grab the following 40 characters
if iStart>0 Then
  sTicket=Mid(sResult, iStart+10, 40)
End If

' Create the new URL with the ticket
sURL = "http://" & sServer & _
  "/QvAJAXZfc/Authenticate.aspx?type=html&webticket=" & _
  sTicket & "&try=" & sSuccessURL & "&back=" & sFailURL

Dim WshShell
' Open iExplore with the generated URL
Set WshShell = WScript.CreateObject("WScript.Shell")
WshShell.Run "iexplore.exe " & sURL, 1

' HTTP Post function using AJAX
Function HTTPPost(sURL, sRequest)
  Dim oHTTP
  set oHTTP = CreateObject("Microsoft.XMLHTTP")
  oHTTP.open "POST", sURL, false
  oHTTP.setRequestHeader "Content-Type", "application/xml"
  oHTTP.setRequestHeader "Content-Length", Len(sRequest)
  oHTTP.send sRequest
  HTTPPost = oHTTP.responseText
End Function
```

 For an example of implementing the ticket request in C#, see a simple example by *Rikard Braathen* at https://github.com/braathen/qv-simple-webticket.

Summary

There has been quite a lot covered in this chapter. We have talked about the different types of **Directory Service Providers (DSPs)** that the Directory Service Connector can use, and we configured and tested several of them. We have enabled the DMS authentication mode and established ACLs in the QMC. We have also seen how to enable third-party authentication by using HTTP headers and Custom Ticket Exchange.

In the next chapter, we will look at monitoring our QlikView Server implementation, and how to troubleshoot issues that might occur.

8
Monitoring and Troubleshooting QlikView Server

Once you have your QlikView Server up and running, you will need to know where to go to monitor and fix issues that might arise.

The first place to start troubleshooting issues will always be the logfiles for various services, and we will review the locations of these files in this chapter.

One place that systems administrators would think of looking, but QlikView administrators might not, is the Windows event log. This will identify the points at which issues with the operating system might be causing a problem.

QlikTech are mindful that it is useful for administrators to have tools to help them with monitoring their system. They have created a **QlikView System Monitor application** that draws data together from various logfiles, to allow you to view information in one place. QlikTech have also released a data governance tool called the **QlikView Governance Dashboard** that uses Expressor technology to scan your implementation for metadata about your documents.

QlikTech have also released a set of free-of-charge power tools that can help you to manage your implementation. We will review these tools in this chapter.

These are the topics we'll be covering in this chapter:

- Locating and interpreting logfiles
- Using QlikView administration dashboards. This includes:
    - ° Configuring and using the QlikView System Monitor application
    - ° Using the QlikView Governance Dashboard

- Using QlikView power tools
- Reviewing the Windows event logs

Locating and interpreting logfiles

Each of the services has its own logfiles in its own folder. In this section, we will locate the files and have a look at the kind of content that you might expect to find in them. We will also examine how to configure the logging options.

Locating the QlikView Server logs

By default, the QlikView Server saves its logfiles to the `ProgramData` folder at `C:\ProgramData\QlikTech\QlikViewServer`. This location can be modified in the **System | Setup | QlikView Servers | Logging** tab.

There are four types of log generated for the QlikView Server:

Log type	Description
Session	This log records useful information about the users' sessions such as connection time, client type, license type. The file is a tab-delimited text file that can be easily read into QlikView.
Performance	On a defined schedule, this log records the current performance statistics for the server. This includes information about the use of memory, active users, active sessions, and so on. Again, this is a tab-delimited text file and can be easily read into QlikView.
Event	This log records events from the QlikView Server such as document loading, **CAL (Client Access License)** usage, server starting, and—most importantly from a troubleshooting point of view—errors and warnings.
Audit	The audit log records the use of QlikView by the users. Not all aspects of usage are recorded, but this log does record user selections, sheet openings, bookmarks and report usages, and maximizing charts (but not just simple use of charts). The **Enable Extensive Audit Logging** option will add details of the selections made within a bookmark.

The **Verbosity** option really applies to event logging. Setting the value to **High** will cause a lot of logging (with potential for server performance impact), including debug messaging.

Once you have completed any troubleshooting, remember to reset the logging to something lower than the **High** setting. Except for the distribution service task logs, logfiles do not get cleared automatically; so, you should remember to clear out any large troubleshooting logs that you have created.

I like to choose to **Split Files** over a period—usually daily—rather than have just one large file. This makes it easier to both find information based on time, and clear out older logfiles.

Locating the Publisher/Reload Engine logs

The default location for the Publisher logfiles in the `ProgramData` folder is `C:\`
`ProgramData\QlikTech\DistributionService\1\Log`. This location can be
modified in the **System** | **Setup** | **Distribution Service** | **General** tab.

Within this folder, you will find several logfiles, as follows:

Log name	Description
YYYYMMDD.log	This is a simple event log that shows information such as the starting and stopping time of the service
LoadBalancer_*.log	This contains the events for the load balancer thread — it is only really useful if you have a clustered Publisher license
WebService_*.log	This contains basic information about task execution
WorkOrder_*.log	This contains information about the triggering of tasks
Root_*.log	This contains the top-level information about the service

Inside the log folder, you will also find a folder with a date stamp for a name, in the
format YYYYMMDD. There will be up to 30 subfolders here (older folders get cleared
out after thirty days). Within each of these folders, there is a subfolder for every
triggered task that the Reload Engine has run. This folder will contain at least one
file `TaskLog.txt`, which is the task execution log. If you have the **Generate Logfile**
option set to **ON** in **Document Properties** for the document that is being reloaded or
distributed (which I recommend!), then a copy of that logfile will also be put in this
folder. You might also find a file called `_InUse.!!!` in one of these folders; this is
present in the folder when the task is currently being executed.

The task log provides you with useful information about the execution of that task
and any errors that might have occurred. If there were script errors, then it will
only give you the information that there was an error, and not what that error was.
However, this logfile will be your first port of call and is the one displayed in the
QMC.

The reason I recommend creating the document log is that if there is a reload script
error, the document log will show you the script error.

Locating the Directory Service Connector logs

The location of the DSC logfiles is, by default, `C:\ProgramData\QlikTech\DirectoryServiceConnector\Log`. There is no option in QMC to change this default location, but in the **System | Setup | Directory Service Connector | General** tab, there is an option to change the level of the logging: **No logging, Normal logging**, or **Debug logging**.

If you want to change the default location, you can edit the `config` file in the Directory Service Connection executable folder (default is `C:\Program Files\QlikView\Directory Service Connector\QVDirectoryServiceConnector.exe.config`), and change the `ApplicationDataFolder` setting.

The log file is useful for troubleshooting any DSP connection errors. As we saw in the last chapter, it also gives information on group resolution for users.

Locating the Management Service logs

By default, QMC logs are saved to `C:\ProgramData\QlikTech\ManagementService\Log`. In the **System | Setup | Management Service | General** tab, you can edit the level of the logging (**No logging, Normal logging**, or **Debug logging**), but not the location. As with the DSC, you can change the `ApplicationDataFolder` setting at `C:\Program Files\QlikView\Management Service\QVManagementService.exe.config`. Note that you can also enable audit logging for the QMC in this `config` file.

The logfile records information about QMC service and errors—especially communication errors with other services. The audit logging tracks the changes made by the users in the QMC.

Locating the web server logs

The web server logs default to `C:\ProgramData\QlikTech\WebServer\Log`. As with other services, you can only change the logging level via the QMC. Again, you can edit the `ApplicationDataFolder` settings at `C:\Program Files\QlikView\Server\Web Server\QVWebServer.exe.config`.

You can also turn on utilization logging for the web service, which records the documents accessed by the web service and the memory configuration. This is most useful if you have multiple web servers.

If you are using IIS, the logfiles will be stored based on a setting in the web server properties. A default folder might be `C:\inetpub\logs\LogFiles\W3SVC1`, or `C:\Windows\System32\LogFiles\W3SVC1`—it depends on the version of IIS.

Using QlikView administration dashboards

QlikTech has released two dashboards to help you manage the implementation. The System Monitor loads the data from the logfiles mentioned earlier and presents the results visually, and the QlikView Governance Dashboard allows you to monitor your data sources and shows you how that data is used.

Configuring and using the QlikView System Monitor application

All of the logfiles have their own format, but all are easily read into QlikView. But wouldn't it be great if someone had already done all the hard work? Well, they have. There is a QlikView application created by the guys in QlikTech Support that reads all of the various logfiles, and creates a dashboard that you can use. This file has gone through many iterations and the most recent version is always available from the QlikView Community, by searching for *QlikView System Monitor*. The most recent version, at the time of writing was v5.0.16, and is available from the following URL:

```
http://community.qlikview.com/docs/DOC-4307
```

The documentation that comes with this application needs to be read before you get going, so that you know what you are doing and what you are looking at.

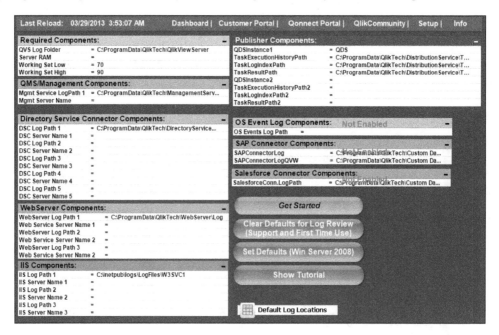

The initial setup screen allows you to point the application at all your different folders. Luckily, there is a **Set Defaults** option that will set up the default folder entry for all of the different services.

 The **Show Tutorial** button is very useful, to help you work out what goes where.

It is worth noting that you can choose to **Clear Defaults** and set up the settings for only one of the services—for example, the QVS Log folder—and just review the data for that service.

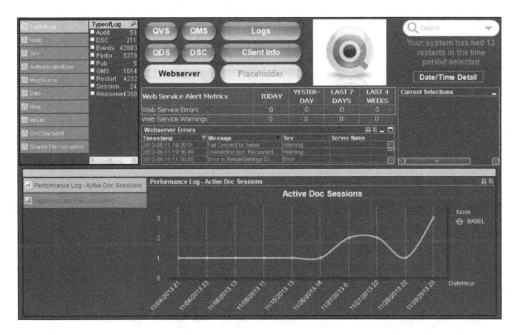

Once the data is reloaded, you can then use the dashboard to view the metrics for each of the different areas. You can, of course, extend the model and add your own charts.

Using the QlikView Governance Dashboard

The QlikView Governance Dashboard is a tool that is available free of charge from QlikTech. It was originally created by the people responsible for Expressor Software, prior to the acquisition of that company by QlikTech.

While not necessarily critical to a QlikView implementation, it is critical if you need to maintain control over the data that are being used by QlikView, and the way that these data are being used. The tool will answer many questions such as:

- What sources are used? What is the lineage of my data?

- How and where are the data used? Which QlikView documents are using which data? What would be the impact of making data changes?

- Which expressions are being used? How many expressions are being used in how many charts and documents? Are they all being calculated in the same way?

When the dashboard is reloaded, it uses the Expressor technology to scan across your entire implementation for data from QVW, QVD, and QVX files.

For more information on the QlikView Governance Dashboard, or to download it for free, go to the QlikMarket at: `http://market.qlikview.com/qlikview-governance-dashboard.html`.

Using QlikView power tools

The power tools are a set of unsupported, free of charge tools that have been created by QlikTech to help you manage your implementation.

The latest versions of the power tools are available from the QlikView Community at: `http://community.qlikview.com/docs/DOC-3059`.

There are 12 tools in all. Some of my favorites are described here.

Server Agent

The Server Agent is an easy-to-use tool that allows you to manage the state of QlikView services on many servers from one location.

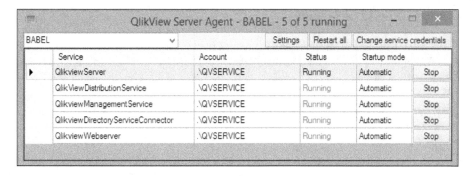

This tool allows you to stop and start services—one at a time or all at once. You can also change the service user for all of the services on one server at one go (which is great, and saves you the trouble of having to change them one at a time).

> You can create a Windows task to start this tool at login; then, it will be available immediately when you need it.

QV User Manager

This is a command-line tool that you can use to manage users outside of QMC. It is good because it allows you to perform bulk updates.

First off, you can perform a simple extract of all your current users:

```
qv-user-manager.exe --list cal > users.csv
```

This is a great way to archive your users, especially when you have many users and you are concerned about the **PGO** corruption (PGO files are the files that contain the license information, and it is known that they can get corrupted from time to time.). I will generally load the resulting file into a QlikView application! You can use this information to create text files that you can use with other user manager switches to re-import users, if they do get lost somehow.

> Because this is a command-line tool, you can easily schedule a Windows task to execute this on a scheduled basis to keep your user list up to date.

SharedFileViewer

Shared files are the files that are located alongside a .QVW file on the server (they will be called Filename.qvd.shared), and are used to store user bookmarks, reports, and collaboration objects.

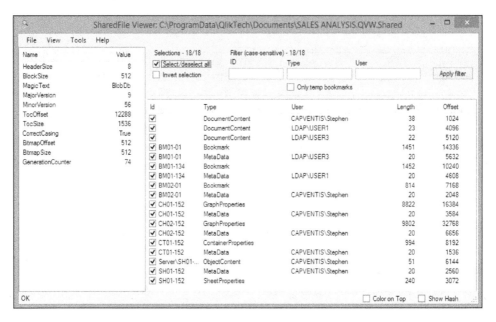

The viewer is a graphical tool that allows you to view the contents of this file (you can't view the charts, just their existence), and perform some useful tasks.

You can export objects and bookmarks to XML files that can be imported into other QlikView applications (they are useful to move server objects into a QVW file).

If the file is very large, there is a possibility of fragmentation. You can view a bitmap of the location of objects in the file and, if necessary, perform a defrag of the file.

Other power tools

There are several other tools, listed as follows:

Tool	Description
QvServerObjectConnector	This is a custom connector that allows you to connect a QlikView document to the shared files, and read their content into QlikView for analysis.
QlikView Server Super Agent	This is a more advanced version of the Server Agent; it can connect to more servers and also send e-mail alerts.
QMS API Client	It is more of a training tool than an admin tool (in my opinion); this can be used to test API calls to the QMS.
QvsDetector	This tool scans your local network for QlikView Servers, and allows you to find out information about them.
Server Object Handler	The object handler is similar to the shared file viewer, except that it goes via the QMS and retrieves the data in such a way that you don't need physical access to the shared file. It allows you to update ownership of objects and has wildcard search options.
Server Object Handler Batch	This has similar functionality to the previous tool, except it is invoked via a command line, which means that it can be scheduled.
XmlDbViewer	This tool allows viewing and editing of the information in an XML-based QVPR.

I recommend you to review these tools and their documentation to see how they might help you in your implementation.

Reviewing the Windows event logs

QlikView runs on the Windows platform; so, it depends on things being correct in the Windows operating system for QlikView to function correctly. If there are problems in Windows, then you could see problems in QlikView that are difficult to troubleshoot just from the QlikView logs. There could be several things that go wrong in Windows, from hardware issues to administrators changing settings, and it is useful to know where to get information about them.

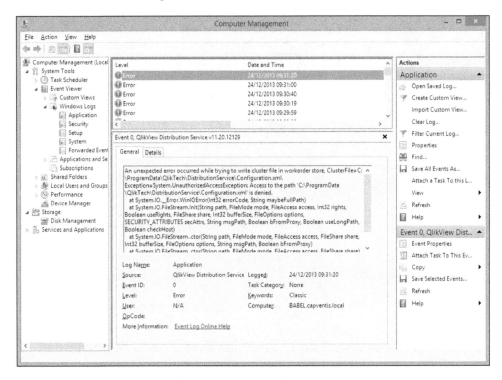

The **Event Viewer** tool is available from **Administrative Tools** or from the **Computer Management** tool. You can also just run the `eventvwr.exe` file.

Any QlikView-related errors will be probably found under the **Application** log area. Depending on how the server is configured, the **Security** logs may also provide useful information. Finally, the **System** log has general errors about the services.

In the preceding screenshot, you can see that the distribution service does not have access to its configuration file. The cause is probably security related, and that is where I would check next. Open Windows Explorer and review the security settings on the file and folder. It may be that an Administrator has "hardened" the system by removing some rights to the `ProgramData` folder!

Summary

In this chapter, we looked at the locations of all of the different QlikView services' logfiles and the information that each of the services contain. We have also seen how to use the QlikView System Monitor to bring these logfiles together into an application that you can use to keep tabs on the implementation. We reviewed a few of the power tools that are useful for managing your system. Finally, we looked at how to find out information from the Windows event logs.

Index

Thank you for buying
QlikView Server and Publisher

About Packt Publishing

Packt, pronounced 'packed', published its first book "Mastering phpMyAdmin for Effective MySQL Management" in April 2004 and subsequently continued to specialize in publishing highly focused books on specific technologies and solutions.

Our books and publications share the experiences of your fellow IT professionals in adapting and customizing today's systems, applications, and frameworks. Our solution based books give you the knowledge and power to customize the software and technologies you're using to get the job done. Packt books are more specific and less general than the IT books you have seen in the past. Our unique business model allows us to bring you more focused information, giving you more of what you need to know, and less of what you don't.

Packt is a modern, yet unique publishing company, which focuses on producing quality, cutting-edge books for communities of developers, administrators, and newbies alike. For more information, please visit our website: www.packtpub.com.

About Packt Enterprise

In 2010, Packt launched two new brands, Packt Enterprise and Packt Open Source, in order to continue its focus on specialization. This book is part of the Packt Enterprise brand, home to books published on enterprise software – software created by major vendors, including (but not limited to) IBM, Microsoft and Oracle, often for use in other corporations. Its titles will offer information relevant to a range of users of this software, including administrators, developers, architects, and end users.

Writing for Packt

We welcome all inquiries from people who are interested in authoring. Book proposals should be sent to author@packtpub.com. If your book idea is still at an early stage and you would like to discuss it first before writing a formal book proposal, contact us; one of our commissioning editors will get in touch with you.

We're not just looking for published authors; if you have strong technical skills but no writing experience, our experienced editors can help you develop a writing career, or simply get some additional reward for your expertise.

QlikView Scripting

ISBN: 978-1-78217-166-9   Paperback: 138 pages

Your comprehensive guide to scripting powerful QlikView applications

1. Understand everything about QlikView, from structuring a script to fixing it to charting object problems

2. Packed full of information and code examples to help you to understand the key concepts and features of QlikView

3. Informative screenshots help you navigate QlikView's scripting menus and dialogs

Instant QlikView 11 Application Development

ISBN: 978-1-84968-964-9   Paperback: 60 pages

An intuitive guide to building and customizing a business intelligence application for your data

1. Learn something new in an Instant! A short, fast, focused guide delivering immediate results

2. Learn how to analyze data for business discovery with QlikView 11 with automatic data linking and wizards

3. Create your own analysis interfaces using tables, lists, and charts

Please check **www.PacktPub.com** for information on our titles

Learning QlikView Data Visualization

ISBN: 978-1-78217-989-4   Paperback: 156 pages

Visualize and analyze data with the most intuitive business intelligence tool, QlikView

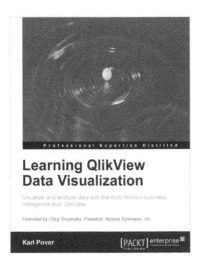

1. Explore the basics of data discovery with QlikView

2. Perform rank, trend, multivariate, distribution, correlation, geographical, and what-if analysis

3. Deploy data visualization best practices for bar, line, scatterplot, heat map, tables, histogram, box plot, and geographical charts

4. Communicate and monitor data using a dashboard

QlikView for Developers Cookbook

ISBN: 978-1-78217-973-3   Paperback: 290 pages

Discover the strategies needed to tackle the most challenging tasks facing the QlikView developer

1. Learn beyond QlikView training

2. Discover QlikView Advanced GUI development, advanced scripting, complex data modeling issues, and much more

3. Accelerate the growth of your QlikView developer ability

Please check **www.PacktPub.com** for information on our titles

www.ingramcontent.com/pod-product-compliance
Lightning Source LLC
LaVergne TN
LVHW081343050326
832903LV00024B/1289

* 9 7 8 1 7 8 2 1 7 9 8 5 6 *